F-105 *WILD WEASEL*
vs
SA-2 "GUIDELINE" SAM

Vietnam 1965–73

PETER DAVIES

First published in Great Britain in 2011 by Osprey Publishing,
Midland House, West Way, Botley, Oxford, OX2 0PH, UK
44–02 23rd St, Suite 219, Long Island City, NY 11101, USA
E-mail: info@ospreypublishing.com
© 2011 Osprey Publishing Ltd

A CIP catalog record for this book is available from the British Library.

Print ISBN: 978 1 84908 471 0
PDF e-book ISBN: 978 1 84908 472 7

Edited by Tony Holmes

Cockpit and gunsight artwork by Jim Laurier
Cover artwork and battlescene by Gareth Hector
Three-views and armament scrap views by Jim Laurier
Page layout by Ken Vail Graphic Design, Cambridge, UK
Index by Alan Thatcher
Typeset in ITC Conduit and Adobe Garamond
Maps by Bounford.com
Originated by PDQ Digital Media Solutions, Suffolk, UK
Printed in China through Bookbuilders

11 12 13 14 15   10 9 8 7 6 5 4 3 2 1

F-105 *Wild Weasel* cover art

On March 10, 1967, the USAF mounted a major attack on the Thai
Nguyen iron and steel works 35 miles from Hanoi. Capts Merlyn
Dethlefsen (pilot) and Mike Gilroy (Electronic Warfare Officer, or EWO),
flying F-105F 63-8341 of the 354th TFS/355th TFW, were involved in
this mission, leading the second element of "Lincoln" flight (a four-aircraft
Wild Weasel flight). Their wingman, Maj Ken Bell, was flying an F-105D.
Both jets were "trolling" for SAMs so that they could attack the site after
first making the operators turn on their "Fan Song" radar. The flight
commander, Maj David Everson (with Capt Don Luna) in "Lincoln 01",
was shot down by AAA and his wingman, Capt Bill Hoeft, had to
withdraw after his jet suffered serious flak damage. Capt Gilroy was able to
locate a SAM site on a pass that left both F-105s damaged, and Dethlefsen
lined up an AGM-45 Shrike missile attack just as two MiG-21s fired at
them from behind. Dethlefsen deliberately flew into heavy anti-aircraft
artillery (AAA) and the MiGs chose not to follow. Seeing a different SAM
site directly ahead, he fired a Shrike at it, putting the radar off the air. On
their next pass both F-105s bombed the site and then returned to strafe it
with 20mm gunfire, leaving much of the target area ablaze. Only then did
the damaged *Weasels* leave after ten minutes in the area. Capt Dethlefsen
was awarded the Medal of Honor for his actions that day, while Capt
Gilroy received the Air Force Cross and Maj Bell the Silver Star.
(Artwork by Gareth Hector using a model supplied by Milviz)

SA-2 "Guideline" cover art

An SA-2 is launched by the 61st Battery of the 236th Missile Regiment on
February 14, 1968, during an attack on the Paul Doumer Bridge. This
unit, commanded by Col M. Tsyganov of the Soviet Army, was the first to
use the SA-2 in North Vietnam. On July 24, 1965, it shot down F-4C
Phantom II 63-7599 of the 47th TFS/15th TFW near Hanoi, thus giving
the SA-2 its first USAF kill. The unit also pioneered techniques such as
manual/automatic "three point" guidance to defeat jamming by US aircraft.
The Paul Doumer Bridge mission on February 14 included an F-105 *Iron
Hand* flight that was following a strike force off the target at 8,000ft,
having kept the SAM batteries quiet during the attack. The 61st Battery's
SA-2 hit F-105D 60-0418 *Sugar Bugger* of the 34th TFS/388th TFW. Pilot
Capt Robert Elliot ejected from the blazing *Weasel* but he did not survive.
His aircraft had been carrying a General Electric QRC-160-8 ECM pod,
later manufactured as the AN/ALQ-87. More powerful than the basic
QRC-160-1 carried by strike F-105s, this "special" pod was tuned to jam
the coded signals "downlink" from the SA-2's FR-15 transponder that
enabled "Fan Song" to track the missile and then send it steering
corrections to its impact point. In the final weeks of 1967 many SA-2s
had lost control due to this jamming. The pod from Elliot's aircraft
was recovered, repaired and studied by Soviet scientists, leading to
modifications to the SA-2's transponder that prevented jamming.
(Artwork by Gareth Hector)

Acknowledgements

I am grateful to the following for their assistance with this book – Col Dan
Barry, USAF (Ret.), Col Mike Chervenka, USAF (Ret.), Maj Murray
Denton, USAF (Ret.), Lt Col Allen Lamb, USAF (Ret.), Nguyen Van
Dinh, Nguyen Xuan Dai, Norman E. Taylor, Pham Truong Huy, Capt Ed
Sandelius, USAF (Ret.) and Dr István Toperczer. Finally, thanks to well-
known Vietnamese writer Thuy Huong Duong, author of *The MiG-17
and Us*, for interviewing Nguyen Xuan Dai and Pham Truong Huy for
this book.

CONTENTS

INTRODUCTION

Pyotr Grushin, who headed the OKB-2 design bureau that conceived the V-750/SA-2 in 1953, would have been surprised that "his" missile was used in Vietnam primarily against tactical fighters. Its original purpose was to intercept high-flying American bombers equipped with nuclear weapons, as Premier Joseph Stalin had considered them to be the biggest threat to the USSR. Only at the conclusion of the Vietnam War was it pitted against the B-52 Stratofortress, the opponent that had motivated Grushin's team 20 years earlier.

Similarly, Alexander Kartveli, a Russian emigrant from Stalin's hometown, Tbilisi, and primary designer of the F-105 Thunderchief nuclear strike fighter in 1952, could hardly have guessed that his creation would evolve into the USAF's first dedicated aircraft for the suppression of enemy air defenses (SEAD), particularly the SA-2, over North Vietnam.

Suppressing anti-aircraft fire was an established mission for tactical aircraft, and its dangers were well known. In support of the massive airborne assault codenamed Operation *Market Garden* in September 1944, four USAAF fighter groups attacked German flak batteries and the 56th FG lost a third of its P-47 Thunderbolts on one mission alone. This role continued through the Korean War and into Vietnam, where anti-aircraft artillery (AAA) was the largest component in the communist North's air defense network. Dueling with flak gunners was risky, officially discouraged, but sometimes inevitable.

The introduction of surface-to-air missiles (SAMs) in the early 1950s demanded new approaches. Radar-directed missiles were seen as the replacement for air-to-air guns, being the nemesis of both manned fighters and bombers. Tests indicated that their probability-of-kill rate was close to 100 per cent even with unreliable thermionic valve technology that existed at the time. The loss of a Lockheed U-2 spyplane over

the USSR in May 1960 and another over Cuba in October 1962 showed the accuracy of the SA-2 and the difficulties in defeating it. Ten years later, America's foremost military aircraft were still being destroyed by the same missile over North Vietnam.

In Korea, the USAF was unprepared for the radar-directed AAA which threatened its B-29 bombers, forcing it to resort to World War II-vintage radar jammers and B-26 Invaders fitted with radar homing. In 1953 the American military responded to the advent of the SA-2 with the funding of urgent electronic warfare research, although fitting SAM warning systems to aircraft like the U-2 still had a low priority.

The Cuban missile threat hastened the development of the Texas Instruments ASM-N-10 (later designated AGM-45 Shrike) as a US Navy anti-radiation missile (ARM) in 1962–64, although it did not appear on USAF aircraft until March 1966. The Bendix Corporation responded quickly to the arrival of SA-2s around Hanoi with a Radar Homing and Warning (RHAW) system proposal for the F-100 Super Sabre that used existing, tested equipment.

By August 1965, after USAF jets began to fall to SA-2s, Brig Gen Kenneth Dempster was tasked with energising the anti-SAM program and finding rapid, operationally practical solutions. His committee recommended a force of hunter-killer aircraft to extend Korean War tactics by using SAM radar detection equipment to identify SA-2 sites rather than merely jamming them.

For Project *Wild Weasel I*, four F-100F Super Sabres carried two systems produced by Applied Technologies – the Vector IV (APR-25) RHAW set with a cathode ray tube strobe showing the direction of a SAM threat, and the IR-133 panoramic receiver which analysed and identified radar emissions. Finally, a WR-300 unit warned of an imminent SAM launch.

The first F-105F-1-RE (62-4412) is seen here sat on Republic's Farmingdale, Long Island, ramp alongside an early F-105D-5-RE for comparison. The latter (58-1155) served as a test aircraft, ending its service career with the 121st TFS ANG. The two-seat F-105 was a minimum-change project that outlived the single-seat variants in frontline service in roles that were very different from its initial training function. (USAF)

5

A camouflaged SA-2 (SA-75M) is prepared for launching near Hanoi in 1967. An open door on the SM-63-1 launcher reveals the cranked handle of the manual back-up traverse system and the large electric motor normally used for elevation and traverse. (via Dr István Toperczer)

As *Wild Weasel* pioneers, Maj Garry Willard and his four-aircraft F-100F Detachment interrupted their training at Nellis AFB due to the urgent need (as seen by the Pentagon) for "an immediate RHAW capability to counter the missile threat" and headed to Korat Royal Thai Air Force Base (RTAFB). Commencing operations on November 24, 1965, the "det" quickly established many of the tactics used by later F-105F/G crews, including the standard SAM evasion tactic – a "split-S" diving turn into the missile's trajectory, with a last-second break that the missile could not follow. Capts Allen Lamb and Jack Donovan made the first of nine SAM-site kills on December 22, 1965, attacking and marking the target with guns and LAU-3 rocket pods for F-105D bombers. Lamb recalled, "As I pulled off there was a bright flash. I must have hit the oxidizer supply for the SA-2 rocket motor".

This engagement introduced a new era of electronic warfare between the crews of the F-100F's successor, the F-105 Thunderchief, and teams of North Vietnamese conscripts and their Soviet advisors. Operating in hot, dark, claustrophobic radar vans, the missile technicians sat close together on simple metal chairs, grappling with the crude but tricky manual control wheels of "Fan Song" guidance radars and learning to penetrate US jamming and countermeasures. They faced the constant risk of an anti-radiation missile strike on their compartment, or a lacerating cluster-bomb attack. Other troops drove the SA-2's cumbersome trans-loader vehicles from the SAM sites into crowded urban areas to collect new missiles once the SAM battery's complement of 12 weapons was exhausted.

In the cockpits of the small numbers of F-105 *Wild Weasels*, pilots struggled to steer their heavy aircraft through unprecedented levels of AAA, not to mention multiple SA-2 launches, trying in poor visibility to identify camouflaged SAM sites and set up missile attacks on them. Their electronic warfare officers (EWOs, or "bears") faced an increasing overload of work as they managed the EW systems and weapons panels. They also had to watch for MiGs, despite the very limited view from their cockpits, and monitor crowded communications and navigation channels, while enduring constant high-g maneuvering. Their mission was neatly summarized in the 388th TFW's Tactics Manual:

> The mission of *Wild Weasel* aircrews generally falls into two roles – *Iron Hand* to suppress and *Wild Weasel* to destroy. Tactics employed on the *Iron Hand* missions are primarily designed to suppress the SA-2 and gun-laying radar defenses of North Vietnam during the ingress, attack and egress of the main strike force. Shrike missiles are used to kill, or at least harass, the SA-2 and/or "Fire Can" (AAA) radar transmitters. Coincidentally the threat represented by the *Iron Hand* flight also diverts the attention of enemy radar operators from the main strike force and this, in itself, is a form of suppression.

On both sides, courage and ingenuity were at least as important as technology.

F-105G-1-RE 62-4428, serving with the 333rd TFS/355th TFW, boasts a conventional bomb load in this May 1970 photograph. The aircraft had received the TCTO 1F-105F 536 blind bombing modification for "Ryan's Raiders"/*Commando Nail* operations that paved the way for many F-105F *Iron Hand* and *Wild Weasel* tactics. It was later upgraded to an F-105G-1-RE. Variously nicknamed *June Bug*, *Rum Runner* and *Red Ball* with the 388th TFW, it completed 5,276 flying hours and ended its days as a gate guardian at RAF Croughton, in Northamptonshire. 62-4428 is the only F-105 presently resident in the UK. (USAF)

CHRONOLOGY

1951

Using German wartime technology, Pavel Kuksenko and Sergei Beria plan the Berkut/S-25 SAM system for Moscow.

1952
September

Republic Aviation Corporation receives an order for F-105A strike fighters.

1953
November 20

To supplement the Almaz-designed S-25 SAM, the Kremlin orders the Fakel S-75.

1955
October 22

First YF-105A flies, followed by the F-105B in May 1956.

1956

SKB P-12 Yenisei ("Spoon Rest") VHF radar enters service in Soviet Union.

1957
November

SA-2 is first shown in public at a Red Square parade in Moscow.

December

S-75/V-750/SA-75 Dvina SAM (SA-2 "Guideline"), with RSNA-75 ("Fan Song") fire control radar, enters Soviet service, with plans for 7,220 missiles.

1959
October 7

Five SA-75 batteries, delivered to the People's Republic of China, shoot down a Republic of China Air Force (RoCAF) RB-57D spyplane for the first-ever SAM kill.

1960
May 1

A U-2C flown by Francis Gary Powers is brought down by a single S-75N, causing a major international incident.

1962
October 27

A 4080th SRW U-2F flown by Maj Rudy Anderson is shot down over Cuba by three SA-2s, precipitating the threat of nuclear war between the USA and USSR.

1962–70

At least 11 RoCAF U-2s are shot down by S-75s over China.

1963
June 11

Two-seat F-105F makes its first flight.

1965
April

Soviet PVO-Strany missile Regiments with SA-75s deploy to North Vietnam. A US Navy RF-8A photographs the first site.

July 24

USAF F-4C Phantom II is shot down by the 236th SAM Regiment near Hanoi. Strategic Air Command U-2s first photograph four SA-2 sites near Hanoi that same day.

Technicians work on prototype F-105F-1-RE 62-4412, which reached Mach 1.15 on its maiden flight (on June 11, 1963) with test pilot Carlton B. Ardery Jnr at the controls. Having performed initial test duties, the aircraft trained pilots with the 4520th CCTW at Nellis AFB from June 11, 1963 until it was lost in an accident near Tyndall AFB, Florida, on January 17, 1966. (Fairchild Hiller/Republic)

An SA-2 creates a huge cloud of dust and smoke as it accelerates away from its SM-63-1 launcher.

July 27	First USAF *Iron Hand* attack mission against SAM sites loses six F-105Ds.
October	First Vector-equipped F-105D tests "anti-SAM" ECM devices, pioneered in the F-100F *Wild Weasel I.*
December 22	Vector-equipped F-105D makes the first SAM-site kill.

1966

February	First of 86 *Wild Weasel III* F-105F conversions is completed.
April 18	AGM-45 Shrike is fired operationally from an *Iron Hand* F-105D for the first time, probably hitting a "Fan Song" radar.
May	Five *Wild Weasel III* F-105Fs deploy to Korat RTAFB, Thailand.
June 7	F-105Fs destroy a GCI radar unit and a "Fan Song" van.

1967

August	SA-2 regiments begin to use optical and "three-point guidance" to defeat USAF jamming.

1968

February	Eight Mod 0 (AGM-78 Standard ARM-capable) F-105Fs are deployed to Takhli RTAFB.

November	Operation *Rolling Thunder* ends but F-105F *Wild Weasels* remain in Thailand to provide EW support for B-52s.

1969

October	61 "Mod 1" updated F-105Fs are re-designated F-105G.

1970–71

	SAM regiments deploy to southern North Vietnam.

1972

April	An F-105G detachment re-deploys to Korat RTAFB and crews subsequently fly *Iron Hand* and "hunter-killer" missions throughout Operation *Linebacker,* remaining in Thailand on active service until October 1974.
December	SA-2 crews down no fewer than 16 B-52s despite comprehensive *Wild Weasel* protection, jamming and chaff countermeasures.

1973

January	Thirty-nine of North Vietnam's 95 SA-2 batteries remain active at the end of the war.

DESIGN AND DEVELOPMENT

F-105F/G THUNDERCHIEF

For the first seven years of the F-105's development and service, its pilots learned to fly the fighter in single-seat versions – the YF-105A, F-105B and F-105D. By 1963 the increasing complexity, weight and cost of these strike variants meant that it had become too hazardous to allow pilots to train wholly on single-seaters. USAF Air Training Command had requested a two-seat F-105B (designated the F-105C) in 1956, but this was cancelled in favor of the F-105E – a two-seat F-105D variant – the following year. The E-model was also cancelled in 1959 as a cost-cutting measure, but in June 1962 an order for 36 F-105Fs was approved, with another 107 planned for Fiscal Year 1963. The latter were financed by cancelling the last 143 F-105D-31-REs.

F-105Fs were intended to fly the same tactical nuclear strike missions as the F-105Ds. This role dated back to 1952 when Republic's Chief Engineer, Alexander Kartveli, adapted his RF-84F Thunderstreak design to carry a small tactical nuclear weapon internally. Evolving slowly via YF-105A prototypes into the F-105B, the type eventually entered Tactical Air Command (TAC) service in 1959. Its massive J75 engine could drive it at 750 knots at ground-hugging altitude with a Mk 28 "nuke" aboard, or almost 1,200 knots at 36,000ft. The 45-degree swept wing spanned only 34.9ft (two feet less than a Spitfire from World War II) against a fuselage length of 63.1ft (similar to that of a C-47 Skytrain). With only 385 sq. ft of wing area to support a 47,000lb take-off weight, the F-105B had limited maneuverability, but offered great stability in its primary strike role. Evading enemy radar via terrain masking, it could outdistance any other fighter at low altitude.

The F-105D proposal in 1957 sought to give all-weather capability, particularly in the European Cold War scenario. A 15-inch fuselage extension allowed a 2,000lb increase in combat weight through the addition of an AN/ASG-19 fire control system, FC-5 flight control system (FCS) and R-14A radar that was optimized for ground mapping. The jet's limited all-weather capability came from the FCS, which permitted both visual and "blind" delivery of conventional and nuclear ordnance. The FCS's terrain guidance mode also enabled the pilot to perform low-altitude navigation in poor visibility. In the cockpit, new vertical tape displays provided basic flight information at a glance. Externally, an arresting hook was added.

In an effort to offset the weight gain associated with these improvements, the aircraft was fitted with a Pratt & Whitney J75-P-19 engine whose water-injection gave it a short-term 2,000lb thrust increase for take-off at increased weight. The M61A1 20mm rotary cannon installed in the F-105B's nose was moved back to accommodate the larger radar, the weapon drawing ammunition from a drum rather than via belts from a box as with the F-105B.

The first F-105D flew on June 9, 1959, and the 4th Tactical Fighter Wing (TFW), which was selected to introduce the aircraft into frontline service, was in business by late 1962. D-models eventually equipped 12 tactical fighter wings before going on to serve with Air Force Reserve and Air National Guard units until 1984.

In order to preserve the range and combat capability of the F-105D, Republic elected to extend its fuselage by 31 inches for the F-105F through the fitment of a "plug" ahead of the air intake line. The two cockpits were given separate canopies and the electronics compartments were moved behind the rear cockpit. The rear fuselage was strengthened and a new vertical stabilizer some five inches taller and 15 per cent larger in area was also added. These changes, together with beefier landing gear components, added 3,000lbs to the overall weight. Nevertheless, the F-105F could fly the same strike missions as the D-model jet, with the front-seat pilot performing most of the mission-related tasks.

Interest in the F-105F as an anti-SAM electronic countermeasures platform began in August 1965 after several US aircraft had been destroyed by SA-2s. However, the scarcity of F-105Fs meant that the more plentiful, though slower, two-seat F-100F was chosen to flight-test equipment for detecting and suppressing SAM sites. In record time, Applied Technologies, Incorporated (ATI) adapted existing ECM devices and produced the Vector IV RHAW set (based on its System 12 for the U-2), the IR-133 panoramic S-band receiver to locate emissions from the SA-2's "Fan Song" guidance radar, and the WR-300 receiver that warned of the imminent launch of an SA-2.

Combat-tested in four F-100Fs, this equipment set, codenamed *Wild Weasel I*, enabled a flight of F-105Ds led by a *Weasel* Super Sabre to destroy a SAM site only five months after the first SA-2 shoot-down of a USAF fighter. However, the IR-133 was susceptible to jamming by USAF EB-66 aircraft operating in the same area and unable to home onto a "Fan Song" while the F-100F was maneuvering energetically. The equipment did not indicate whether the aircraft was being tracked by a SAM either.

As part of their dominant role in the air war over North Vietnam, F-105D and F-105F Thunderchiefs attacked SA-2 sites as soon as permission was granted to do so. In this typical 1970 scene at Takhli RTAFB, Lt Col Jack Spillers, commanding the 355th TFW's 357th TFS, begins a take-off roll in the relatively spacious single cockpit of F-105D 62-4229, named after his wife. Note that the Mk 83 1,000lb high explosive bombs attached to the jet's center pylon have been fitted with fuze extenders. (Mrs J. Spillers via Norman Taylor)

Republic Aviation had already tested an AN/APS-107 RHAW in an F-105D but rejected it in September 1965 in favor of the Vector IV as an urgent means of reducing the escalating attrition amongst Thunderchief units over North Vietnam. ATI and the Sacramento Air Material Area (SMAMA) successfully completed an installation in F-105D 62-4291 within five days, and a second aircraft was ready on 27 October 1965. This F-105D (61-0138) was fitted with a Bendix DPN-61 homing receiver, a fin-cap radar-warning receiver (RWR) and a SAM threat warning CRT display as the

When the first F-105Fs arrived at Korat in May 1966, their function was so secret that few on the base knew the meaning of the term *Wild Weasel*. Both of the Thai-based Thunderchief wings struggled to keep the temperamental, largely experimental *Weasel* equipment functioning in the heat and humidity of Southeast Asia. The F-105F's high combat weights strained landing gear, tires and braking parachutes, and five aircraft were lost after malfunctions in these components. Water injection system failure on take-off also resulted in several close calls. F-105F 63-8321, seen armed with a pair of Shrikes while serving with the 357th TFS, later flew with the 6010th WWS at Korat, bearing the nicknames *Sawadee Krud* and *Miss Lucky*. The aircraft survived until it crashed during an attempted emergency landing at NAS Point Mugu, California, on March 2, 1978. (USAF)

F-105G THUNDERCHIEF

F-105G-1-RE 63-8336 *PATIENCE* of the 17th WWS/
388th TFW in February 1973. This aircraft entered
service as an F-105F with the 23rd TFW in
September 1964, and in March 1968 the jet went
to war as a single-seat *Combat Martin* jammer
aircraft with the 388th TFW at Korat RTAFB,
although it actually flew most of its missions in
a strike or *Iron Hand* role. Transferred to the 355th
TFW in May 1969, 63-8336 then served with the
18th TFW at Kadena AB, prior to being flown back
to the USA and placed in storage under 23rd TFW
management at McConnell AFB. Converted to
F-105G configuration in 1972, the aircraft returned
to the war torn skies of North Vietnam with the
17th WWS for Operation *Linebacker I*. The
Thunderchief continued to fly *Wild Weasel* missions
from Korat RTAFB until October 1974, when it was
transferred to the 35th TFW and thence to ANG
units and final storage at Davis-Monthan AFB in
April 1982, with more than 4,000 flying hours on
record.

20ft 5in.

34ft 9in.

67ft 0in.

first attempt to equip the jet for the SEAD role under project *Wild Weasel II*. This included F-105F 62-4421 using the AN/APS-107, the US Navy's AN/ALQ-51 and external QRC-160-1 jamming pods.

The project was quickly replaced by *Wild Weasel III*, which focused solely on the F-105F with the AN/APR-25 (Vector IV), AN/APR-26 (WR-300, conceived by ATI's Bill Doyle) and IR-133 – basically the *Wild Weasel I* suite. It was initiated on January 8, 1966 by Brig Gen Kenneth C. Dempster, who headed the USAF Anti-SAM Task Force from August 13, 1965. His brief from the outset had been to develop effective systems for tactical aircraft that allowed them to protect themselves from radar-directed weapons. A primary objective was the evolution and speedy deployment of fast hunter-killer teams to locate SA-2 sites using *Wild Weasel* detection aircraft and destroy them with *Iron Hand* F-105Ds equipped with 2.75-inch rockets, bombs and 20mm cannon. Republic and SMAMA had quickly modified the prototype F-105F (62-4416) to serve as the *Wild Weasel III* test-bed by February 3, 1966, and work began on six more F-105Fs while the prototype started a hasty test program at Eglin AFB.

The speed of the latter caused numerous quality control and technical problems with the installations, particularly the AN/APR-25, which failed to equal its performance in the F-100F because of inadequate co-axial cabling. With an imminent deployment to Korat RTAFB looming for five of the Thunderchiefs, all seven aircraft were re-worked and re-tested repeatedly, while six more F-105Fs were re-fitted in May 1966. An additional system was installed to help pilots locate SAM sites, particularly when they were well camouflaged. This ATL AE-100 system used a pattern of small antennas around the F-105F's nose to receive azimuth and elevation information on an emitting "Fan Song" and display it so that a pilot could establish the direction of the threat radar. Delays in installing this gear, and in testing the rival AEL Pointer III system and the QRC-317 SEE-SAMS threat detection and evaluation system, meant that the five *Wild Weasel III-1* aircraft could not fly to Korat until May 28, 1966.

Although SEE-SAMS was initially rejected, development continued by North American Aviation and an improved SEE-SAMS B variant was evaluated in the Korat aircraft. In a period of experimentation with evolving ECM technology and tactics, together with the frequent development of relevant new products by the US defense industry, the *Wild Weasel* F-105s received constant modification so that each aircraft soon had minor differences from the rest.

At Korat and Takhli RTAFBs the *Weasels* expanded the tactics pioneered by *Wild Weasel I* F-100F crews, although they initially continued to use the F-105F as a pathfinder/flight leader for three F-105D bombers on *Iron Hand* hunter-killer operations. With the adoption of the US Navy's AGM-45 Shrike ARM from March 1966, however, the F-105F could now also make stand-off attacks on "Fan Song" radars rather than merely marking them with 2.75-inch rockets for F-105D bombers.

The employment of the Shrike also changed the role of *Weasel* crews during 1966–67, for missile-equipped F-105s could now suppress SAM batteries simply through their mere presence, forcing a "Fan Song" team to shut down rather than attract a radar-homing missile. It was no longer necessary to risk life and limb physically knocking out an SA-2 site with bombs and/or rocket projectiles.

Another batch of 18 F-105Fs was pulled out of the training program from July 1966, these jets being fitted with ER-142 receivers operating in the E-G frequency bands in place of the IR-133 – the new receiver displayed its information on two panoramic cockpit scopes. The ER-142 was in turn superseded by the ER-168 (AN/APR-35), installed with the AN/ALT-34 jamming system. An improved SEE-SAMS set (eventually re-designated AN/ALR-31) boasting additional wing-tip antennas was installed in a number of F-105Fs in 1968.

Various built-in jamming systems, including the US Navy's AN/ALQ-51 deception jammer, were tested to provide anti-SAM protection. All F-105s operating over North Vietnam were required to carry jamming protection, but pylon-mounted QRC-160-1/8 pods used up a weapons station and could interfere with the *Wild Weasel* equipment. The solution to this problem came in the form of "split" AN/ALQ-101 pods, attached to either side of the lower central fuselage, housing QRC-288 (later QRC-335) jammer components. As the AN/ALQ-105, this system equipped the ultimate Thunderchief *Wild Weasel*, the F-105G.

The jet's most important enhancement was the provision of AGM-78A Mod 0 Standard ARM capability. This weapon – another US Navy initiative – had a warhead three times larger than the Shrike's and a range three times greater than its 12-mile radius. The latter meant that aircraft could now fire an ARM from outside the effective range of an SA-2. And while the Shrike had to be launched almost directly at its target, the Standard ARM could be made to turn up to 180 degrees before homing on a

Iron Hand flights often included single-seat, Shrike-armed F-105Ds led by an F-105F whose crew would tell them when to launch the missiles. This 469th TFS F-105D (58-1161, seen in May 1966) was hit as Capt Buddy Bolden pulled out of his bomb-release dive over Route Pack 6 on November 22, 1966. Unaware that his aircraft was on fire, Bolden headed for Korat, crossed the Thai border and ejected seconds before the F-105 exploded. The two QRC-160 pods that it carried were in such short supply that they were recovered and the surviving parts were rebuilt by General Electric into one very reliable pod. (USAF)

hostile radar. If that radar was turned off (which would cause a Shrike to break lock and fail), the AGM-78 used a memory circuit to log the last known position of the radar signal and continue to head towards it.

Fourteen F-105Fs were modified to carry the AGM-78 from September 1967, and eight of these entered combat from Takhli in early March 1968. A year later the ECM suite was radically updated to handle the AGM-78A Mod 1 missile and, in due course, the AGM-78B. Retaining only the AN/ALT-34 jammer and AN/ALR-31 (SEE-SAMS), the new installation used an AN/APR-35 panoramic receiver and AN/APR-36/37 sensors in place of the AN/APR-25/26. New missile control panels, a tape recorder and a tracker to feed back information on the missile's flight in order to estimate its likely success rate were also installed. Deliveries of revised "Mod 1" aircraft began in January 1969, and the jets' success in combat persuaded the USAF to standardize all surviving F-105F *Weasels* as Mod 1 airframes, re-designating them F-105Gs. With the addition of 12 new conversions, this placed 61 F-105Gs in the active inventory. They all received the AN/ALQ-105 suite in due course too, although a few F-105Gs entered combat before these external fuselage pods were added.

In this guise the F-105 *Wild Weasel* fought through the final stages of the Vietnam War in 1971–73, out-performing its intended replacement, the F-4C Phantom II *Wild Weasel IV*. The latter lacked AGM-78 capability, and from 1966 onwards never reached the standard of electronics systems reliability achieved by the F-105G.

SA-2 (S-75) "GUIDELINE" SAM

In March 1946 Gen Carl Spaatz, commanding the US Army Air Forces, asserted that "Strategic Air Command will be prepared to conduct long-range offensive operations in any part of the world". The success of heavy bombers during World War II had demonstrated their devastating power. Post-war, Strategic Air Command (SAC) acquired 2,042 jet-powered B-47 Stratojets and then 744 B-52 Stratofortresses capable of delivering nuclear weapons at 550kts over a 3,000-mile combat radius.

Faced with the formidable task of defending its vast land area against both this threat and high-flying US spyplanes, the Soviet Union urgently promoted a new generation of interceptor fighters, but for the defense of its cities another layer of protection was required that would be more effective than fighters or guns. In 1945 Soviet scientists used captured data from German surface-to-air guided missile projects to design first-generation SAMs, but internal political competition prevented their completion. By 1951 Joseph Stalin had instigated a new project, codenamed *Berkut*, which surrounded Moscow with SAM batteries and radars connected by ring-roads. The first batteries were declared operational in 1956, using the V-300 (NATO codename SA-1 "Guild") missile conceived by fighter designer Semyon Lavochkin.

A second, mobile system was needed for the protection of wider areas of the Soviet Union, and in November 1953 the Almaz design bureau's Boris Bunkin headed a team that conceived the S-75, with Lavochkin-trained Pyotr Grushin as principal designer.

SA-2 (S-75) "GUIDELINE" SAM

An SA-2/S-75 Dvina missile depicted on an SM-63-1 Launcher. The latter's folding outrigger "feet" stabilized the launcher base, which could also be fitted with four wheels for transportation. Motors rotated the launcher through 360 degrees and raised it for missile firing, usually to an angle of around 60 degrees.

35ft 1in. (missile only)

Two parallel versions of the missile system were drafted, the SA-75 Dvina using the low-frequency ten-centimeter wavelength N-band for its radar systems and the S-75N Desna with the higher-frequency six-centimeter V-band. The missile component was designated V-750, or Item 1D (SA-2 "Guideline" in NATO terminology). It used a command guidance system in which the two-stage missile was steered within a narrow radar beam radiated by an Almaz RSNA-75 "Fan Song" fire control radar after the target had been acquired and tracked by the much wider "vision" of a P-12 Yenisei ("Spoon Rest") search radar and a PRV-11 ("Side Net") height-finding radar. The latter could operate at a range of up to 110 miles, while "Spoon Rest" (or the P-15 "Flat Face" C-Band radar) was effective for up to 175 miles. For early versions of the missile the "Spoon Rest" unit was preceded by the P-8 Dolphin ("Knife Rest A") or P-10 ("Knife Rest B") radars. "Fan Song" operators could launch and guide up to three missiles almost simultaneously within a 40-mile radar range.

Missile mobility was provided by a special trans-loader/semi-trailer towed behind a ZIL-157 tractor. Rounds were loaded directly from the trailers onto their single-rail launchers, the latter usually being arranged in a star-shaped pattern of six launchers surrounding the radar and support vehicles.

North Vietnam's SAM site patterns followed the strict Soviet star or "flower" shape, and their heavy AAA was also positioned Soviet-style in rings, firing in rotation. Situating the batteries close to populated areas increased the problems for US pilots. As this photograph graphically shows, the only clear attack route for aircraft targeting the SAM site was from the northeast, directly over a AAA emplacement. All other routes into the battery were blocked by nearby housing. Missiles were assembled by the regiment's technical battalion, which also kept the SM-63-1 launchers well-maintained. Soviet supervisors often complained that some batteries handled their missiles carelessly or fired them without proper guidance procedures in a wasteful manner. [USAF]

After the weapon system had been successfully tested (from April 1955), up to 1,000 SA-2 sites, each with a six-launcher battery, were established across the USSR between 1957 and 1965. The system was relatively easy to operate with minimal training. SA-2s replaced 100mm KS-19 and 130mm KS-30 anti-aircraft guns at many locations around cities, military research facilities, industrial areas and government administration centers. Low cost and comparative simplicity made the system suitable for supplying to most Warsaw Pact countries, as well as China and North Korea and, eventually, more than 35 other nations across the globe. The SA-2 remained in service in Iraq during Operation *Desert Storm*, and as recently as 1993 a Georgian Army "Guideline" is thought to have destroyed a Russian Su-27 "Flanker" over Abkhazia.

The Soviet method of deploying SA-2 batteries was adopted by most other users, including North Vietnam. A regiment consisted of three battalions, each controlling six SM-63-I launchers, their support radars and other equipment.

The commencement of Soviet over-flights by U-2s and other spyplanes in 1956 prompted the rapid development of the improved Item 11D (V-750V) SA-2 variant capable of reaching almost 85,000ft, while the more powerful Item 13D (V-750VN) had been developed by 1958. This was joined in Soviet service by the S-75N Desna (V-750VK/ SA-2B) in 1959. However, it was the Item 11D that became the standard export version of the missile to Soviet allies, including North Vietnam.

U-2 flights across Warsaw Pact territory commenced on June 20, 1956 with CIA Project *Aquatone*, which lasted for ten days. A number of these flights saw aircraft penetrating Soviet airspace. In July some of the rumored SAM sites around Moscow were photographed for the first time, and although the U-2 was detected on Russian A-100 radar, the SA-1 missiles were not prepared for launching. President Dwight D. Eisenhower authorized these early, revealing flights but suspended them when it became clear that Soviet forces were consistently tracking the U-2s on radar, and might well respond with SAMs.

The CIA opened a new route from Turkey and Pakistan through thinner Soviet radar cover, and during these sorties U-2s photographed early tests of the SA-2 missile and "Fan Song" radar (originally nicknamed "Fruit Set") at a range near Lake Balkhash. Having repeatedly failed to down a U-2 with interceptors for almost four years, Soviet PVO (Air Defense) forces finally achieved their aim on May 1, 1960. Their quest to destroy a U-2 equated in urgency to North Vietnam's desire in later years to bring down a USAF B-52 bomber.

Flying U-2C 'Article 360' from Peshawar on May 1, Francis Gary Powers overflew SA-2 batteries at the Tyuratam missile-testing center, but operators received inadequate warning to start their generators and acquire the target on radar. A fuzed "Fan Song" radar circuit at the Chelyabinsk SA-2 regiment resulted in another failed launch a short while later, while a series of MiG and Sukhoi interceptors, with orders to ram the U-2C, tried unsuccessfully to reach Powers' 70,500ft altitude. However, near Sverdlovsk, Maj Mikhail Voronov's "Fan Song" operators detected the U-2C at 14 miles, and three S-75N Desnas (Item 13Ds) were fired in automatic mode. Although

An SA-2 site photographed by an RF-101C on August 16, 1965, shortly after the first USAF loss to a SAM on July 24. The frequent movement of batteries to alternative sites meant that the usual earth revetments, or "berms", were not built high enough to offer much protection. These missiles retain their factory-applied light gray heat reflective paint. (USAF)

BAMBOO MATTING

RADAR

only one launched successfully, it was enough to destroy the aircraft when its 3,600 warhead fragments shredded the spyplane's rear fuselage.

The capture of Powers caused a major international crisis, and the Kremlin learned much about US airframe and engine technology from the wrecked aircraft. Over-flights of the USSR were suspended, but by then the PVO had received valuable experience to help it develop better coordination and reliability for its SA-2 regiments that would also benefit other users, including North Vietnam.

The next stage in the evolving confrontation between Soviet SAMs and American technology began on September 15, 1962 when US electronic intelligence (ELINT) picked up "Spoon Rest" emissions from Mariel, in Cuba. These indicated that SA-2 missiles were ready to engage American reconnaissance aircraft searching for SS-4 and SS-5 ballistic missiles, MiG-21 fighters and Il-28 "Beagle" bombers that Soviet Premier Nikita Khrushchev had placed on the island following the CIA's failed "Bay of Pigs" attempt to unseat Cuban President Fidel Castro. The USSR had also supplied 144 SA-2 launchers and PVO crews from April 1962, providing comprehensive SAM

The heart of the V-750/SA-2 system was the RSNA-75M "Fan Song B" missile control radar. The massive horizontal Lewis scanner (with a parabolic UHF dish antenna attached) and the similar vertical unit were transported separately when the missile battalion moved sites, sometimes to rough-hewn locations in the jungle to intercept B-52s. Although the USA had acquired captured Soviet radars from Israel in 1967, its first working "Fan Song" came via Indonesia in the late 1960s. (Dr István Toperczer)

RSNA-75M "FAN SONG B"

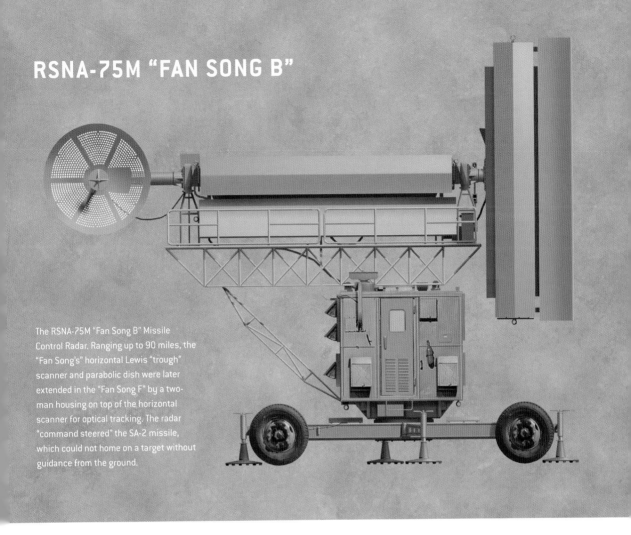

The RSNA-75M "Fan Song B" Missile Control Radar. Ranging up to 90 miles, the "Fan Song's" horizontal Lewis "trough" scanner and parabolic dish were later extended in the "Fan Song F" by a two-man housing on top of the horizontal scanner for optical tracking. The radar "command steered" the SA-2 missile, which could not home on a target without guidance from the ground.

coverage for the whole of Cuba. On October 27, 1962, 4080th Strategic Reconnaissance Wing U-2F 56-6676, flown by Maj Rudolph Anderson, was destroyed by three 507th Anti-aircraft Missile Regiment SA-2s fired at a range of six miles from a site near Banes.

Secretary of Defense Robert McNamara was dissuaded from his plan to launch 500 bombing sorties against the SA-2 sites in response to the shoot-down. Instead, Ryan Model 147 drones, feeding data to *Common Cause* RB-47 'Strato-spy' aircraft, were deployed to try and detect the SA-2's fuze activation signals so that ECM protection for US jets could be devised. No more missiles were fired, but it became clear that the unauthorized shoot-down had resulted from a lack of coordination between the SA-2 commander and higher Soviet command in Cuba. With the world at the brink of nuclear war, the crisis ended the following day when Khrushchev ordered a withdrawal of Soviet weapons and personnel from Cuba, although many SA-2s and their upgraded S-band "Fan Song A" radars remained.

Thanks to CIA photogrammatic analysis of the first SA-2s seen during Moscow military parades, the USAF was able to construct a model SA-2 and then test it at Tullahoma, Tennessee. The results of these tests, combined with data gleaned from captured missiles, allowed US pilots to develop a high-g maneuver in an effort to evade the weapon – the U-2 was unable to maneuver so drastically. The SA-2's uplink, downlink and radar proximity fuzing codes were not obtained until February 13, 1966, when a *Blue Spring/United Effort* Ryan Model 147E drone from Bien Hoa AB was shot down by two SA-2s near Hanoi seconds after re-transmitting the relevant data to a USAF RB-47H. It was, in the Assistant Secretary to the Air Force's opinion, "the most significant contribution to electronic reconnaissance in the past 20 years".

Duels between U-2s and SA-2s continued, particularly over China where RoCAF "Black Cat" U-2s and Takhli RTAFB-based "Det G" U-2Fs established how SA-2 operators had learned to use AAA fire control radars (undetectable by the U-2's radar warning system) to track the Lockheed spyplanes before handing them over to the "Fan Song" controllers when they got to within 22 miles of the latter. Missiles could then be launched eight seconds later. Such techniques would be further refined by the North Vietnamese, who again used AAA radar to assist with SAM targeting. For example, during Operation *Linebacker II*, U-2R pilots were tasked with watching and counting the SA-2s fired at B-52s after they had already been targeted by flak. On December 26 Capt 'Fuzzy' Furr observed 84 missiles in all from his U-2!

Whereas Cuba and many other Soviet client states were provided with later versions of the SA-2 such as the 13D Desna and 20D Volkhov with its more "jam-proof" RSN-75V2 "Fan Song", the North Vietnamese were only allowed the basic Dvina version during the war years, partly because the Kremlin feared that the Chinese (no longer on good terms with the USSR) would acquire and copy the technology as they had done with MiG fighter designs. Although there were plans to introduce the S-125 Neva (SA-3 "Goa"), with superior low-altitude performance, none were in Vietnamese use by war's end, despite frequent American reports to the contrary.

The SA-3 would have been more effective against the tactical strike aircraft that were North Vietnam's main aerial adversary until 1972, so would the later "Fan Songs" that operated on shorter wave-lengths and gave superior target resolution.

Lacking major technological upgrades, the North Vietnamese and their Soviet mentors concentrated on improving and adapting tactics. Mainly, these involved camouflaging their missile sites, limiting the use of "Fan Song" emissions to defeat American ECM and radar-homing missiles and employing their equipment's full range of operating frequencies to bypass jamming. One small but vital change was the provision of a "dummy load plug" (normally used for testing purposes) that "drew off" most of the "Fan Song's" 600 kW radiation in the form of heat, even when it was operating at full power. Rather than waiting for the radar's thermionic valves to warm up after it had been switched off to escape counter-measures, the "Fan Song" could go instantly to full power to track a target and launch SA-2s within the 30 seconds needed to ensure the optimum kill potential.

"Fan Song's" very narrow tracking beam was accompanied by a strong radar signal that was picked up by RWR equipment in the F-105, as was the change of signal to a "three ring" indication on the *Weasel's* cockpit scope that signified an imminent launch. A pilot could then attempt to avoid the missile, although this usually meant jettisoning his bombs or other external ordnance. Jamming the "Fan Song's" signal was

obviously a more effective counter-measure, and the heavy losses to SA-2s and radar-directed AAA throughout 1966 caused Gen Bill Momyer (deputy commander for air operations, Military Assistance Command, Vietnam) to order extended trials at Takhli with QRC-160-1 pod-equipped F-105s flying ahead of strikes from September 26 through to October 8. In response to this change in tactics, SA-2 crews concentrated on the un-podded F-105s instead.

Initially, two pods were carried per F-105, but shortages resulted when the pods proved successful and both Thai-based Thunderchief wings wanted them for all missions over North Vietnam. Trials at Eglin AFB showed that single pods would suffice if "pod formation" was flown by each F-105 flight, with correct 1,500ft spacing and positioning between aircraft to maximize the jamming effect and the addition of blanket jamming by EB-66C/E *Brown Cradle* aircraft.

Although the early pods, designed for one-off nuclear strike usage, were rather fragile and unreliable, they presented the most serious impediment to the "Fan Song B" element in the SA-2 "kill chain". The capture of a QRC-160-8 (ALQ-87) ECM pod following the shoot-down by an SA-2 of Capt Bob Elliot's 34th TFS F-105D (60-0418) on February 14, 1968 enabled Soviet technicians to quickly modify the SAM's FR-15 transponder so that it could not be jammed. This duly increased the vulnerability of many B-52s to SA-2s during Operation *Linebacker II*.

A less technically advanced upgrade came with the RSN-75V2 "Fan Song F" modification that allowed daylight SA-2 operation despite intense ECM. A small cabin was fixed to the top of the "Fan Song's" horizontal antenna to house one or two observers. Using an electro/optical sight to detect targets in daylight and fair visibility, the system "slaved" the radar scanner to the optical sight via servo motors. This in turn permitted radar tracking and missile guidance to successfully take place at altitudes down to 300ft.

Caught in a strike-camera frame, an F-105 turns hard to evade an SA-2. American pilots discovered that the "Guideline" was capable of tracking aircraft targets flying as low as 200ft, but its true forte was intercepting high-flying bombers – as SAC was reminded during *Linebacker II*. Battery commanders were allocated their targets by Hanoi's Air Defense Headquarters on the basis of information from P-12 early-warning radars. The batteries then picked up the target on their "Spoon Rest" radars, transferring it to the "Fan Song" at closer range. (USAF)

23

TECHNICAL SPECIFICATIONS

F-105 *WILD WEASEL*

As the USAF's first major SEAD aircraft, the F-105F/G enabled its crews to establish operational techniques for countering SAMs that were vital during the Vietnam conflict and still remain valid today.

Designed as a strike fighter to fly very fast, low and straight, the F-105 had the speed to duel with SAMs, although it lacked the agility in this role enjoyed by its successors like the F-4G and F-16D Block 50. It was 100mph faster than the F-100F *Wild Weasel I* (which tested the initial *Wild Weasel* electronics package operationally), however, thus allowing the F-105F/G to approach targets at low altitude at the same 500+ knots speed as the F-105Ds or F-4 Phantom IIs that accompanied it as bombers. The Thunderchief's small wing and powerful Pratt & Whitney J75-P-19W engine enabled the aircraft to out-run all Vietnamese Peoples' Air Force (VPAF) fighters – with the possible exception of the MiG-21MF– at low altitude.

The J75 powerplant was a development of Pratt & Whitney's very reliable JT-3/J57 turbojet, designed in 1949 and crucial to the success of the first three "Century Series" fighters, the North American F-100, McDonnell F-101 and Convair F-102, as well as Boeing's B-52, 707 and KC-135, among others. The engine also powered the two YF-105A prototypes. More than 21,000 J57s had been built by 1959 when Pratt & Whitney enlarged it by replacing the first three low-pressure turbine stages with two more powerful fan stages. The new engine was designated the J75. Power with

afterburning increased from 16,000lbs thrust to 26,500lbs with water injection, and fuel economy was also improved, although it still burned JP-4 at almost 1,000lbs per minute at full thrust! The engine was fed by innovative forward-swept, variable-area intakes with moveable "plugs" and bleed-air doors to regulate the air volume at different airspeeds to avoid stalls.

In early service with F-105 units the 20ft long engine sustained a series of fires. This problem was solved by providing the jet with additional cooling ducts in the rear fuselage. Although the J75 usually proved to be tough and reliable, in combat, engine

Like many other 1950s fighters, the F-105 had a removable rear fuselage for access to the engine. This had the added advantage that damage to a rear fuselage could be repaired while the aircraft flew missions with a rear section borrowed from another F-105. In this photograph 388th TFW maintainers manhandle a massive J75 engine on an awkward-to-maneuver Model 400A hydraulic support trailer. (Fairchild-Hiller/Republic Aviation)

25

failures continued to be the second most common cause of F-105 losses next to battle damage. This was partly because the engines were often run at their maximum thrust for long periods, but losses declined after engine modifications in 1968.

The F-105 introduced numerous groundbreaking technological innovations, and like the J75, some of these took several years to get right. Probably the most troublesome element of the aircraft's avionics was its complex General Electric ASG-19 Thunderstick fire control system. Indeed, its low serviceability rate earned the F-105 a poor reputation amongst USAF maintainers. Thunderstick offered radar search and ranging functions for visual and "blind" bombing, as well as an air-to-air interception mode.

Modification programs for the aircraft, including 29 major updates in 1967 alone, increased survivability. One of these, the pilot recovery system, was a response to the many combat losses caused by the F-105's highly vulnerable hydraulic system. Designed for missions where small-arms fire was not anticipated, the system had hydraulic lines located along the aircraft's belly. Combat had quickly revealed that even modest battle damage to a line usually resulted in a rapid loss of control as the fluid drained away and the stabilator moved to an unrecoverable pitch-down position.

From 1967, a cockpit switch activated a lock to secure the stabilator in the neutral position, allowing the pilot a little more time to fly to a safer area using his throttle and flaps to provide limited control. A further system introduced an emergency hydraulic reservoir pressurized by a ram-air turbine to give pilots a chance of safe recovery to base. Lines for this system ran in a new fairing above the rear fuselage.

The aircraft's normal General Electric FC-5 automatic flight control system gave the option of stability augmentation in manual control or fully automatic mode for toss-bomb delivery and landing approaches.

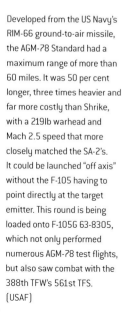

Developed from the US Navy's RIM-66 ground-to-air missile, the AGM-78 Standard had a maximum range of more than 60 miles. It was 50 per cent longer, three times heavier and far more costly than Shrike, with a 219lb warhead and Mach 2.5 speed that more closely matched the SA-2's. It could be launched "off axis" without the F-105 having to point directly at the target emitter. This round is being loaded onto F-105G 63-8305, which not only performed numerous AGM-78 test flights, but also saw combat with the 388th TFW's 561st TFS. (USAF)

CBU-52/58 cluster bomb munitions were feared by SA-2 troops as they were able to shred the soft-skinned "Fan Song" and its support vehicles, as well as the missiles themselves. Combined with AGM-45 and AGM-78 missiles, cluster bomb units could devastate SA-2 sites. In a particularly successful operation on October 6, 1972, three hunter-killer teams destroyed two sites, seriously damaged three others and added a possible "Fan Song" kill with CBU-52/58s and anti-radiation missiles. Using a common SUU-30H dispenser, these units weighed between 790lbs and 820lbs each. They contained 217 BLU-61A (CBU-52B) or 650 BLU-63A (CBU-58) explosive sub-munitions, each the size of a large orange and weighing between one and three pounds. (USAF)

WILD WEASEL ARMAMENT AND ELECTRONICS

Two-seat Thunderchiefs retained the M61A1 20mm rotary cannon and five weapons stations of the F-105D. The centerline and inboard pylons were plumbed for fuel, with a 450-gallon or 650-gallon centerline tank and a 450-gallon tank on each inboard pylon. Internal fuel amounted to 1,135 gallons, with a further 390-gallon tank occupying the internal bomb-bay. Typical F-105F/G weapons options included six 500lb Mk 82 low-drag general purpose bombs or five CBU-24/B canisters replacing the centerline tank, one or two AGM-78 Standard ARMs (F-105G only) replacing fuel tanks on the inboard wing pylons and either AGM-45 Shrikes or single cluster bomb units on the outer pylons. If AGM-78s were loaded, they also required special General Dynamics LAU-80 pylons. Each missile, with its pylon, weighed 1,600lbs.

A shortage of ordnance pylon space was a problem for the *Weasel* mission, particularly when crews were ordered to carry the QRC-160-1 jamming pod on all missions over North Vietnam in early 1967. The pod not only used up a pylon, it also interfered with the *Wild Weasel* ECM equipment.

The two cockpits, each fitted with a Republic-designed rocket-powered ejection seat, were essentially similar to the F-105D version, with full flight instrumentation and some armament controls repeated in the rear pilot's "office". F-105Fs sometimes operated as single-seat bombers to make up F-105D numbers, and ten were modified as single-seat *Combat Martin* aircraft with an AN/ALQ-59 communications jamming system replacing the rear seat. Their purpose was to jam VPAF MiGs' ground control intercept (GCI) signals, although they seldom if ever performed this role in combat. All of these aircraft were later re-fitted as F-105Gs.

Changes to the *Wild Weasel* ECM packages in the F-105F and early F-105G airframes throughout 1966–68 resulted in the rear cockpits being frequently modified. The standard F-model engine and flying control panels were increasingly replaced by

F-105 GUN

The General Electric T171 cannon fitted in the nose of the F-105 revived a late 19th century design which added an electric motor to a "Gatling" rotary, multi-barrel gun. It entered production as the M61A1 in 1957, and its compactness, light weight and firing rate of up to 6,000 rounds per minute made it ideal for the F-104 Starfighter, F-105 Thunderchief and later fighters. In the F-105D, F and G, its 1,028 rounds of linkless 20mm ammunition (allowing about ten seconds of firing) were stored in a drum that also collected empty shell cases. The hydraulically-powered gun weighed 275lbs – little more than half the weight of a full ammunition load.

F-105 MISSILES

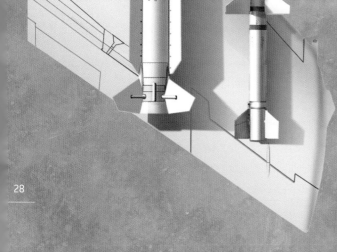

Up to four Texas Instruments AGM-45 Shrikes could be carried by the F-105, although the usual load was two. The ten-foot long, 390lb AGM-45A/B – the world's first dedicated anti-radiation missile – was produced in 21 sub-variants, distinguished mainly by minor changes in their guidance sections and seeker heads. Its 147lb warhead and 18-mile effective range were limiting factors. Nevertheless, more than 18,500 were produced between 1963 and 1982. The appreciably larger General Dynamics AGM-78 Standard ARM was manufactured for the US Navy and USAF from 1967 through to 1978, the 15ft-long weapon boasting a 215lb warhead. A shortage of AGM-78s and the F-105's high fuel consumption when carrying the bulky weapon resulted in typical ordnance loads of a single Standard and two Shrikes per jet, with a 450-gallon fuel tank "balancing" the AGM-78 on the opposite wing pylon. Although more effective than the Shrike, the Standard's overall success rate was still only around the 20 per cent mark.

Between April 1 and September 30, 1972, F-105Gs launched 230 AGM-78s, although there was a failure rate of more than 25 per cent in the first two months that led to a temporary "grounding" of the missile. Rocket motors were also sometimes cracked in transit, causing premature detonation – motors were x-rayed on delivery thereafter. The smaller AGM-45 proved to be quite difficult to discard in an emergency, as it lacked an explosive jettison system for either the missile or its pylon. (USAF)

displays and controls for the AN/APR-35, AN/APR-36 and AN/ALR-31, while the introduction of the AGM-78 missile required the installation of another control panel and 14-channel tape recorder. Key components were the IR-133 display that provided indications of "Fan Song" activity.

The AN/APR-25/26 sensors "read" the SA-2's signals, enabling the pilot to home onto "Fan Song" emissions. The system's cockpit display included a yellow "launch" light to show that an SA-2 was headed towards the F-105. Within the correct range and with the aircraft pointed at the threat emitter, an AGM-45 Shrike could pick up

The standard bomb-load for F-105D/Fs throughout much of the war was six or eight 750lb M117 bombs, although CBU or "slick" Mk 82 bombs were often more effective against SAM sites. This 469th TFS/ 388th TFW flight is bombing "straight and level" above clouds early in 1967 – one of the most likely ways to attract a SAM that allowed insufficient time for the F-105s to avoid it. 62-4325 crashed near Korat when the flight control system failed during a test flight on March 14, 1967. (Lt Col Jack Spillers via Norman Taylor)

the radar signal, lock onto it with its own seeker and home onto the target when launched. With the definitive F-105G and its QRC-380 and AN/ALQ-105 jamming systems, a further panel was added. Both cockpits had similar control columns, but ordnance delivery was usually the responsibility of the front seat occupant, leaving the rear seat "Bear" to monitor the various ECM displays and keep the pilot informed on threats from radars, missiles or MiGs.

F-105G Thunderchief *Wild Weasel* Specification

Powerplant	Pratt & Whitney J75-P-19W rated at 24,500lb st (afterburner only)
Dimensions	
Wingspan	34ft 9in.
Length	67ft 0in.
Height	20ft 5in.
Wing area	385 sq ft
Weight	
Empty	31,646lbs
Loaded	54,580lbs
Performance	
Max speed	1,390mph at 36,000ft
Range	391 miles in combat configuration
Service ceiling	43,900ft at combat weight
Time-to-climb	28 minutes to 30,000ft at combat weight, maximum military power (this compares with a time of 11.6 minutes for a bombed-up F-105B!)
Armament	One M61A1 20mm cannon
	Two AGM-78 Standard anti-radiation missiles

SA-2 "GUIDELINE"

Designated the V-750 (sometimes V-75) Dvina in the Soviet Union, the missile is better known in the West as the S-75 or by its NATO name, SA-2 "Guideline" Mod 0. Evolved from the 1944 German Wasserfall missile concept, the weapon was designed to protect the strategic and population centers of Russia, but it soon became the primary and longest-serving air defense missile offered to the Soviet Union's allies too. Several variants were developed, including the short-lived experimental V-753 that was to be fired from an eight-round magazine aboard *Sverdlov* Class cruisers. Developed quickly in the mid-1950s, the missile was designed to intercept targets at medium to high altitude. Its performance against aircraft below 3,000ft was poor.

The two-stage SA-2 had a Kartukov PRD-18 booster section with 14 tubes of NMF-2 solid chemical propellant (more in later versions) and large fins to impart stable flight on launch. This burned for four to five seconds and then fell away, leaving the Isayev S2.711 sustainer motor to maintain flight at Mach 3. The latter burned hypergolic liquid propellant comprising TG-02 (50 per cent isomeric xylidine, 48.5 per cent triethylamine and 1.5 per cent diethylamine), with AK-20 fuming nitric acid as the oxidizer. This specification was derived from the Wasserfall.

A turbo-pump was required to supply the motor with OT-155 Isonite (isopropyl nitrate) liquid fuel sufficient for a 22-second engine burn. The later Item 20D Volkhov development of the S-75 used a different fuel comprising 56 per cent kerosene and 40 per cent Trikresol, with a TG-02 "starter fuel" supply to ignite the mixture. This was much safer to handle and store than the volatile mix used in the Dvina or Desna ("Guideline Mod 1") models. For the North Vietnamese, a shortage of technicians qualified to perform these tasks meant that fewer than 40 missiles could be assembled and filled with fuel, oxidizer and compressed air daily.

SA-2 RADAR AND SUPPORT EQUIPMENT

The majority of the system's low-cost electronic elements were housed in its ground-based support vehicles. Within the missile's 35.1ft body was the 5E11 Schmel or 5E29 radio proximity fuze, using either "strip" antennas on the external skin or a dielectric radome. Theoretically, the missile was accurate to within about 210ft, and the proximity fuze would be armed and programmed within that range via two waveforms within the command uplink channel. Alternatively, there was a simple impact fuze and a command fuze that could be used to detonate the warhead from the ground. The warhead itself was comparatively large to increase the chance of a kill from a "near miss" position. In its V-88 version the warhead weighed 420lbs and contained 8,000 metal fragments that would be ejected at a rate of 7,000ft per minute over a lethal diameter that could vary between 200ft at lower altitude and 800ft above 35,000ft.

The rocket exhaust deflector at the rear of the SM-63-1 launcher reduced ground erosion when a SAM's booster motor was ignited. Stabilizing outrigger "arms" on the main unit folded for transportation. When SA-2s first appeared in North Vietnam in 1965, Assistant Secretary of Defense John T. McNaughton told Gens William Westmoreland and Joseph Moore, who were in charge of the US war effort and wanted to attack the sites, "You don't think the North Vietnamese are going to use them? Putting them there is just a political ploy by the Russians to appease Hanoi". (via Dr István Ioperczer)

A hit by only a handful of these on an F-105's hydraulic or fuel systems could cripple the aircraft.

The guidance system relied on three components – a command link receiver, an autopilot and a radar beacon at the rear of the missile to provide a tracking signal to the "Fan Song" guidance radar. The command link receiver operated with four pulse-modulated waveforms. Two of them supplied climb or dive and left/right turn commands to the missile's powered steering fins after the booster was ejected. The other two provided programming and arming signals to the radio proximity fuze.

Missiles were transported on purpose-built, two-wheeled "transloader" semi-trailers pulled by a ZIL-157 tractor unit. An SA-2 could be transferred from the transport rail on the trailer to its SM-63-1 launcher by five men without additional lifting equipment. The launch rail of the SM-63-1 was lowered to the horizontal position and the missile on its transport rail was swung out at 90 degrees to the trailer. When the two rails were positioned end-on to each other the 5,042lbs SA-2 was simply slid backwards from one to the other by basic manpower and the relevant electrical connections were made, all within 10–15 minutes.

The SM-63-1 launch rail could be elevated up to 80 degrees and rotated through 360 degrees on a turntable – both the launch rail and the turntable were powered by electric motors housed in the launcher's base unit. The "transloader" could be fitted with four wheels for quick transfer to another site. In launch position the rail rested on a foldable cruciform base with a movable blast deflector that would be lowered just before firing to reduce ground erosion from the exhaust.

An RF-101C Voodoo captures its own shadow in a reconnaissance photograph of a SAM site. All of the SM-63-1 launchers visible in this remarkable shot have their wheels attached, indicating either recent arrival or imminent departure. SA-2 components were easily tow-transportable, and the many cables linking the units could be re-laid rapidly. Missile soldiers often ensured that these sites escaped detection through the skilful employment of camouflage netting and foliage, as well as the erecting of temporary hut-like structures. They also frequently moved location. The presence of SAMs forced USAF and US Navy pilots that were searching for them to fly below 1,500ft AGL to avoid missiles, thereby placing themselves squarely within range of groundfire that varied in size from hand-held rifles and AK-47s to dedicated AAA batteries. (USAF)

SA-2 (S-75) "GUIDELINE" SAM CUTAWAY

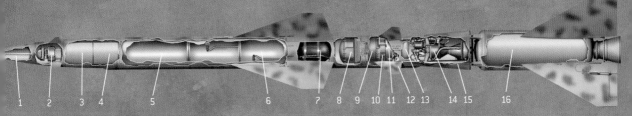

1. Radio proximity fuze transmit antenna
2. FR-15 Shmel radio proximity fuze
3. V-88 high-explosive fragmentation warhead
4. Radio proximity fuze receive antenna
5. AK-20F oxidizer melange tank
6. TG-02 propellant tank

7. Compressed air tank
8. AP-75 autopilot module
9. FR-15Yu command link module
10. Battery
11. Transducer
12. Cruciform controls

13. OT-155 Isonate turbopump gas-generator propellant tank
14. Isayev S2.711V rocket engine
15. Adapter fairing
16. PRD-18 boost powerplant with 14 tubes of NMF-2 propellant

The launch process began with early warning of an incoming raid from high-powered, low-frequency radars such as the massive A-band P-14 "Tall King". An SA-2 battalion's own search radar was the P-12 Yenisei ("Spoon Rest"), although the P-15 ("Flat Face") search and track set and PRV-11 ("Side Net") height-finding radar were also available.

Development of the VHF P-12 was commenced in 1954 by the SKB Bureau and culminated in the P-12NP in the 1970s. It could be retuned quickly to four pre-set frequencies and detect targets at 100–150 miles using 12 Yagi antenna elements that displayed their information on two scopes – an "E-scope", showing the target's height, and a plan position indicator.

Resistance to jamming and interference was steadily improved throughout the 1960s. "Spoon Rest-A" used two adjacent ZIL trucks, with the antenna array mounted on one and the radar indicators in another. Later versions such as the P-12NP separated the antenna into a remote trailer that could be located at a safe distance of up to 1,600ft from the operating unit. ARMs then homed on the antenna rather than the radar cabin.

Having acquired a target, "Spoon Rest" passed its range, bearing and altitude data to the RSN-75 "Fan Song" radar vans via land lines. Four vehicles were required for most versions. The radar antennas were mounted on the "PV" van, which also housed the transmitters. The battery commander and up to five operators with their command consoles were housed in the "UV" van. An "AV" cabin contained other tracking and transmitter equipment, while electrical power was generated by diesel motors in the "RV" van.

"Fan Song" had two functions – target acquisition of up to six targets and missile guidance of up to three SA-2s against a single target. Its operators refined the battalion "Spoon Rest's" data to establish the exact position and flightpath of the target aircraft, as well as calculating an impact point ahead of the target or as close as possible to it.

Members of a missile regiment run to their operational positions past spare rounds that are ready on their trans-loaders for each launcher. Assembling and fueling an SA-2 took several hours' work, personnel having to handle hazardous substances in urban warehouse depots that were eventually targeted in the latter stages of *Linebacker II*. Camouflaging the missiles (as seen here) caused them to absorb heat, which could in turn damage the weapons' internal electronics. (Author's collection)

After launching, they then tracked both the target and the missiles' transponder beacons – three SA-2s could be launched at a single target at six-second intervals. In automatic mode the radar computer calculated course corrections once the missile had been "captured" in the "Fan Song's" narrow guidance beam and its spent booster had dropped away. This capture had to happen within about six seconds of launching otherwise the missile went ballistic and self-detonated after 60 seconds.

Detonation near a target via the proximity fuze was indicated by a light on the "Fan Song" consoles. The narrow radar beam (only 7.5 degrees wide and 1.5 degrees in the scanning direction even in the upgraded "Fan Song E") also limited the extent of maneuvering commands via the radio uplink in case the missile strayed beyond the bounds of the "Fan Song's" guidance emissions. This gave US pilots their best chance of evading a missile, if they saw it in time. However, the computer could rapidly generate and transmit new steering commands if the target turned to a new course. To counteract jamming or the threat of anti-radiation missiles, the SA-2 crew could resort to manual modes without using the "Fan Song's" guidance. Although this increased the missile's reaction time for maneuvering, it required considerable skill to be effective.

Almaz SA-2/S-75M "Guideline" Specifications
Dimensions

Length	35.1ft
Diameter (widest)	2.1ft
Span (widest fins)	8.2ft
Weight	5,040lbs
Engine thrust (sustainer motor)	6,834lbs
Booster rocket thrust	up to 110,000lbs

Performance

Max speed	Mach 3
Max/min lethal range	18 miles/5 miles
Max/min lethal altitude	85,000ft/1,500ft

THE STRATEGIC SITUATION

In 1964, with American involvement in Vietnam escalating into direct rather than covert military intervention, the USAF's primary doctrine of strategic bombing remained much the same as it had been in 1945. President Lyndon B. Johnson's request for plans to attack North Vietnam produced an air force list of 94 targets for strategic bombing attacks that would have quickly removed that country's limited industrial, transportation and military structures had they all been attacked. It was assumed that this in turn would negate the North Vietnamese desire to take control of South Vietnam and neighboring countries.

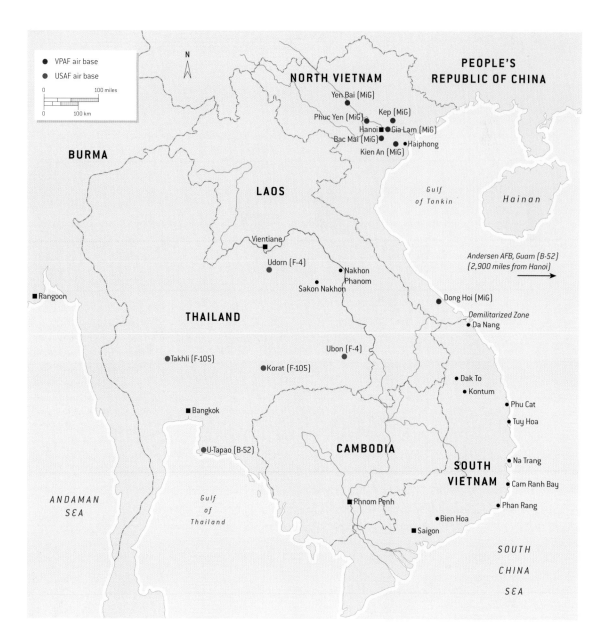

Legend:
- VPAF air base
- USAF air base

0 ——— 100 miles
0 ——— 100 km

NORTH VIETNAM

PEOPLE'S REPUBLIC OF CHINA

Yen Bai (MiG)

Phuc Yen (MiG)   Kep (MiG)

Hanoi ■ ● Gia Lam (MiG)

Bac Mai (MiG) ●   ● Haiphong

Kien An (MiG)

BURMA

LAOS

Gulf of Tonkin

Hainan

Vientiane ■

Udorn (F-4)

Nakhon Phanom

Sakon Nakhon

Andersen AFB, Guam (B-52)
(2,900 miles from Hanoi) →

■ Rangoon

Dong Hoi (MiG)

Demilitarized Zone

THAILAND

● Da Nang

Ubon (F-4)

●Takhli (F-105)

●Korat (F-105)

● Dak To

● Kontum

● Phu Cat

■ Bangkok

● Tuy Hoa

●U-Tapao (B-52)

CAMBODIA

ANDAMAN SEA

Gulf of Thailand

SOUTH VIETNAM

● Na Trang

● Cam Ranh Bay

■ Phnom Penh

● Phan Rang

● Bien Hoa

■ Saigon

SOUTH CHINA SEA

Wild Weasels served with the 355th TFW at Takhli RTAFB, in Thailand, from mid-1966, although its F-105s moved to Korat RTAFB in September 1970. Here, they joined other Thunderchiefs that had flown from Korat with the 388th TFW since April 1967.

Originally, the attacks were to have been delivered by the B-52s of SAC, which, under Gen Curtis E. LeMay, had sustained the concept of massive atomic retaliation as the USAF's *raison d'être*. The strike fighters of TAC (led by Gen Otto Weyland) had also assumed a nuclear role since the mid-1950s.

The politicians insisted on very limited, conventional warfare responses instead, so B-52s were held back from North Vietnam for seven years. The attack task instead fell to strike fighters such as the F-100 Super Sabre and F-105 Thunderchief, which were generally unsuited and unprepared for World War II-style "iron bomb" raids. As Gen John Vogt (deputy commander for air operations, Military Assistance Command, Vietnam) commented in 1972, "The USAF did not have an all-weather bombing

capability. This was a nemesis in the *Rolling Thunder* campaign". During the monsoon season, from November to March, "the enemy had almost a sanctuary". Nevertheless, from February 24, 1965 to October 31, 1968, the USAF flew more than a million sorties and dropped 750,000 tons of bombs in its longest-ever bombing campaign, Operation *Rolling Thunder*.

Rather than intervening directly, as many feared they would, the Soviet Union and China agreed to North Vietnamese Premier Pham Van Dong's 1964 requests for MiG fighters, SAMs and anti-aircraft artillery, together with the radar and technical expertise to operate them. In March 1965 the Pentagon anticipated the imminent delivery of SA-2s as a response to *Rolling Thunder* attacks and the possibility of B-52 strikes – the missile had of course been designed specifically to oppose the latter. By mid-1966 North Vietnam had a full, Soviet style, integrated air defense system centered on Hanoi, which soon boasted the most heavily defended airspace in the history of aerial warfare.

New Yorkers Majs John Revak and Stan Goldstein reckoned they were among the last *Wild Weasel* crews during the *Rolling Thunder* period to complete 100 missions. Seen here with CBU-armed F-105F *Dragon III*, their assigned aircraft in 1968 was actually 62-4424 *Crown 7* of the 44th TFS. Revak and Goldstein flew their 100th mission – an *Iron Hand* for a RESCAP operation over North Vietnam – in 63-8306 *Bad SAM*. Assigned to Majs Dornberger and Carver at the time, this aircraft later participated in the Son Tay rescue mission. (USAF)

And there was no shortage of personnel to man the missile sites and AAA batteries, as around 100,000 men reached military service age annually. At its peak during the 1972 *Linebacker* raids, the SA-2 element of the North Vietnamese integrated air defense system numbered 36 missile battalions and nine technical battalions split between nine Air Defense Missile Regiments.

American pilots faced both 85mm and 100mm heavy AAA at altitudes up to 39,000ft, 37mm and 57mm guns at medium altitude and almost "wall-to-wall" 23mm and small-arms fire below 5,000ft (where most losses to AAA occurred). More than half of the 2,300 heavier caliber AAA weapons were located within 30 miles of central Hanoi. Many were radar-directed and could be moved fast to guard almost any potential target.

An SA-2 explosion hangs in the air behind a speeding F-105, which appears to have sustained damage from the proximity-fuzed missile. The introduction of QRC-160 ECM pods cut the losses to SA-2s and radar-directed AAA dramatically. Carrying pods limited F-105 four-ship flights to 15 degrees of bank and around 2,000ft spacing between element members, however. Although this protected Thunderchiefs against SA-2s, the rigid formations made them tempting targets for MiGs. "Fan Song" operators would hope to engage aircraft that had been separated from the pod formation, or during their individual dive attacks on the target. Fortunately for the USAF the North Vietnamese were not given the SA-2E version of the "Guideline", which was far more resistant to pod jamming. (USAF)

Ironically, far more US tactical aircraft were shot down by AAA guns protecting SAM sites than by the missiles themselves, small-caliber AAA accounting for around 85 per cent of the US aircraft losses during *Rolling Thunder*. However, the threat of SAM hits at altitudes above 1,500ft forced aircraft to enter the lethal range of most AAA, while the need to evade an oncoming SAM usually forced a pilot to jettison his ordnance load, effectively aborting his mission.

Despite the Cuban experience, the USAF was comparatively ill-prepared in 1965 to tackle SAM and radar-directed AAA threats, and it did not expect to face them over North Vietnam. The basic technology was well understood, thanks in part to a copy of the SA-2 manual obtained through the spy Oleg Penkovsky in 1960 and via electronic intelligence of SA-2s in Cuba. Development work had begun on the QRC-160 jamming pod for tactical aircraft to carry externally, the EB/RB-66 detection/jamming aircraft and SAM launch-warning devices, the first of which were installed in *Trojan Horse* U-2s overflying Hanoi in 1965. However, many in Washington, DC and the Pentagon assumed that the threat of US air power would be enough to deter Vietnamese insurgency. Indeed, the appearance of SAM sites did not at first convince President Johnson's civilian advisors, including Robert McNamara, that the Russians would actually allow them to be used against US aircraft. The Joint Chiefs of Staff, on the other hand, unanimously advocated immediate destruction of the first sites.

In fact, the SA-2 represented the most important advance in the establishment of a comprehensive North Vietnamese air defense system, a process that had begun in October 1963 with the merger of the VPAF with radar and AAA batteries under the overall command of Col Gen Phung The Tai. When US air attacks began, Soviet Premier Alexei Kosygin visited Hanoi, and thereafter Pham Van Dong proved adept at making the Russians and Chinese vie with each other in supplying modern air

An impressive pre-deployment line-up photograph of 2061st Missile Regiment SA-2s on their trans-loaders near Hanoi. This unit claimed the destruction of F-4E 68-0314 from the 308th TFS/31st TFW on June 27, 1972 as it flew a straight-and-level chaff bombing mission near Gia Lam airport in Hanoi. (via Dr István Toperczer)

defense equipment, in particular SAMs and MiG-21s from the USSR and MiG-17 and MiG-19 copies made by Shenyang in China, totaling 65 fighters by August 1966.

The appearance of SAM sites prompted demands from the Joint Chiefs of Staff for decisive retaliation against them, including a B-52 night attack and the bombing of MiG airfields. Opinion was divided over whether the Soviet Union and China would respond in kind to this action. On one hand the State Department believed that Chinese fighters might even intercept US jets over Hanoi, while the CIA felt that there would be no risk of this kind of intervention. President Johnson delayed, fearing casualties to Russian and Chinese advisors at the sites, but accepted foreign policy advisor William Bundy's proposal that they should be bombed "if they are used to inflict significant losses on us".

The North Vietnamese relied heavily on Soviet personnel providing them with technical expertise for the operation of their missile batteries. Almost 17,000 of them worked at SAM sites and other defense installations from April 1965 onwards, and four were killed in action.

Initially, North Vietnamese SAM crews were trained in the Soviet Union, and subsequently at ten centers in Vietnam, but the first operational SA-2s were manned by PVO-Strany personnel from Russia commanded by Gen G. A. Belov and Col G. Lubinitsky. Col Tsyganov had the first operational regiment, the 236th, in place near Hanoi by July 1965, and three other regiments, manned largely by Russians, were in service by the end of 1966. Each regiment commanded four launch batteries, with six launchers per battery. When Lubinitsky's site fired on an F-105 escort flight of four "Leopard" F-4C Phantom IIs from the 47th TFS on July 24, 1965, one was destroyed. Capt Roscoe Fobair was killed and Capt Richard "Pop" Keirn, a former Eighth Air Force B-17 pilot and World War II PoW, entered captivity once again. SAM warnings from a nearby RB-66 had not been received by the crew in time to take evasive action. Two other aircraft were downed by the same site later that month.

A typical hunter-killer element comprising F-105F 63-8329 (lead jet) with Shrikes, CBUs and a centerline fuel tank and an F-105D wingman carrying six Mk 82 LDGP bombs and wing tanks. The F-105F, variously named *Rosemary's Baby* and *Protestor's Protector/My Diane*, was escorting an RF-4C Phantom II that photographed a remote SA-2 site near Mu Ron Ma on January 28, 1970. When fired upon by AAA, the *Weasel* crew (Capts Richard Mallon and Robert Panek) retaliated, but were shot down by ground fire. In the rescue attempt that followed, two MiG-21s downed an HH-53 helicopter, killing its six crew, while the *Weasel* crew appear to have been executed by their captors. (USAF)

In the summer of 1972 there were reports of a new missile dubbed the "Black SAM" that was capable of defeating the *Weasel's* ECM equipment. US Intelligence personnel in-theater believed that the weapon was the SA-3 "Goa". These rumors probably started after a number of camouflaged SA-2s were seen in reconnaissance photographs. Lending credence to the reports was the fact that "Fan Song" operators were now routinely making frequency changes while tracking targets. No SA-3s were received until late 1972, however. The North Vietnamese sometimes complained that their SA-2s were refurbished, obsolete stock sourced by the USSR from other Soviet client states. Nevertheless, some SA-2 sites acquired almost mythical status, including VN-549, which was incorrectly credited with five B-52s destroyed prior to it being knocked out by a *Weasel* hunter-killer team on December 29, 1972. (via Dr. Istvan Toperczer)

This loss resolved the Johnson administration's doubts about Soviet policy in deploying the missiles, and it also prompted urgent redress to protect American aircrews. With 16 squadrons of tactical fighters, five tactical reconnaissance units and 21 EB/RB-66 electronic warfare aircraft scheduled to deploy to Southeast Asia by the end of 1966, the potential losses to SAMs could easily be foreseen. This was particularly true of the two F-105D/F Thunderchief tactical fighter wings based at Takhli and Korat RTAFBs in Thailand, which were responsible for the majority of the *Rolling Thunder* bombing missions over North Vietnam.

A solution for their self-protection was soon available through Project *Problem Child* at Eglin AFB, where Lt Col Ingwald Haugen devised a four-ship "pod formation" for tactical aircraft. In October 1965 tests, each F-105 carried a pair of General Electric QRC-160-1 D/E band jamming pods tuned to defeat the "Fan Song's" track-while-scan emissions. Their combined jamming power protected the formation from a missile lock-on apart from a brief period when it was directly over the site.

Sadly, Pacific Air Force policy-shapers regarded the pods as unreliable and a wasteful use of two of the F-105's five weapons/fuel pylons, so a delivery of QRC-160-1s was soon returned to the USA. After very heavy losses of F-105s in the summer of 1966, further combat trials were ordered, and by October the pods became an essential, highly effective addition for all F-105 missions to North Vietnam. Thunderchief losses to radar-directed AAA and SAMs fell from 72 in the "pre-pod" six months to 23 in the six months following their introduction.

The second potential remedy proved far more difficult to implement. Following the July 24, 1965 Phantom II shoot-down, SAM site attacks were finally allowed, but such strikes in the first three days after the incident cost no fewer than six F-105s. It was in inauspicious beginning for a seven-year, cat-and-mouse war between the Thunderchief and the SA-2.

THE COMBATANTS

While the first North Vietnamese SAM troops were training in the USSR in 1965, Soviet PVO-Strany crews established and operated the country's missile batteries. Having also formed ten training units around Hanoi, Soviet supervisors controlled the battalions for at least two years, causing some resentment among Vietnamese troops.

Battalions honed their skills on Firebee drones and later, at very much higher altitudes and unsuccessfully, on the A-12 and SR-71 reconnaissance aircraft that identified around 150 SA-2 sites soon after they began over-flights in November 1967. U-2 missions over North Vietnam were discontinued when the SA-2 regiments became operational.

North Vietnamese Dvina trainees in the USSR found difficulty with both the language and the heavy emphasis on ideology and inflexible discipline. Instructors insisted on the "three missile salvo" tactic – the first to make the target aircraft maneuver and thereby lose energy, making it an easier target for the second or third SA-2. Soviet advisors continued to refine their techniques throughout the war. For example, new anti-Shrike tactics included activating two "Fan Songs" briefly so that the missile would pass between them, while for the AGM-78, several "Fan Songs" were turned on and then simultaneously switched off, confusing the missile.

For *Linebacker II*, the nine SA-2 regiments and others recalled from the south were concentrated in Hanoi's 361st Air Defense Division and around Haiphong. Their effort was directed in 1972 by Soviet Col-Gen Anotoliy Khyupenen. Faced with the B-52's formidable jamming power, operators were told to use multiple launches at single targets so that the bombers' EWOs, jamming each threat individually, were overwhelmed. Crews were also trained to launch SA-2s manually, only engaging "Fan Song" guidance in the final 15 to 20 seconds of the missile's flight.

Khyupenen conceded that, "The missile crews were inadequately trained to fight when jammed and under aerial attack. Fearing anti-radar missile strikes, the launch

crews tried to fire at the B-52s without turning on their radars at all, which prevented them from detecting targets under jamming and switching to manual guidance". He reported that only three B-52s were hit by missiles that had been actively guided – the norm was manual guidance, with automatic tracking for the last few seconds. In his estimation 64 SA-2s detonated too far from their targets, some on the metallic chaff used to mask the bomber formations. Most successful firings used at least two missiles. Several B-52s were hit as they made their post-bombing turn away from the target. As they banked, the intensity of their jamming was reduced, allowing canny "Fan Song" operators a rapid lock-on.

F-105Gs were vulnerable too. The last *Weasel* loss (63-8359) of the war, on November 16, 1972, was escorting B-52s near Thanh Hoa when a SAM site fired. Maj

LEO K. THORSNESS

Like fellow *Wild Weasel* Medal of Honor winner Merle Dethlefsen, Leo Thorsness was born a Mid-West "farm-boy" in the early 1930s and chose to fly fighters after receiving his pilot's wings. Both men flew the F-100 Super Sabre before transitioning to the F-105 and being posted to Takhli RTAFB in 1966. As Col Jack Broughton, Vice Wing Commander of the 355th TFW told the author, "At Takhli I had a super-smart, aggressive good guy *Weasel* leader in Leo Thorsness. We were almost always short on *Weasel* aircraft and crews. I wanted one *Weasel* guy to manage the assets and call the shots".

Thorsness arrived at Takhli in the second batch of *Weasel* crews soon after the first five F-105Fs had been lost in just 45 days in July–August 1966. He was determined to try new tactics, which included flying the *Weasel* missions at higher altitudes – around 18,000-20,000ft – in order to reduce the loss rate. With his regular "Bear", ex-B-52 EWO Capt Harold E. Johnson, Thorsness also pioneered the idea of splitting the *Weasel* flight into two elements, with an F-105F and an F-105D in each pair, as a way of doubling the potential SAM-site attacks.

On April 19, 1967, Thorsness and Johnson, in F-105F 63-8301, were lead "Kingfish" *Weasels* for an attack on the Xuan Mai barracks near Hanoi. The second "Kingfish" element was jumped by MiG-17s, and Majs Thomas Madison and Thomas Sterling were forced to eject from F-105F 63-8341 – Dethlefsen's Medal of Honor mission aircraft. "Kingfish 1" completed its bomb-run and set off to cover the *Weasel* crew as they parachuted down. Both "Kingfish" F-105Ds were also damaged and had to withdraw, leaving Thorsness's F-105F as the only American aircraft in the area. Noticing a MiG-17 that was about to make a strafing run on Madison and Sterling, Maj Thorsness shot it down and then out-ran a second MiG-17.

Low on fuel, he headed for a tanker, called in a RESCAP team for the downed *Weasels* and briefed them on the situation, and on SAM evasion tactics as they were dangerously near Hanoi. After a brief discussion with his "Bear", Thorsness then returned to provide solo cover for his wingman. En route they encountered a "wagon wheel" formation of five MiG-17s, and Thorsness fired out his last 500 rounds at one, scoring a probable kill. The other four immediately pursued him, and he dived in afterburner to weave through several valleys, sometimes flying below 50ft as he shook off the VPAF fighters.

Meanwhile, another MiG-17 flight had shot down the lead RESCAP A-1E "Sandy" aircraft (flown by Maj John Hamilton) and Thorsness returned to the fight once again, advising Hamilton's wingman to turn hard just above the forest to evade the MiGs. Although out of ammunition, the F-105F crew turned hard into the MiG-17s, denying them a target and allowing "Sandy 02" to escape. Low-altitude maneuvers in afterburner had run the F-105F low on fuel again and Thorsness sought another tanker, feeling that the rescue had failed since contact with the downed crew was impossible.

In his brief absence the "Brigham Control" rescue coordinator had directed "Panda" (a post-strike F-105 flight) into the rescue area, where its leader, Capt William Eskew, had shot down a MiG-17 – two other VPAF fighters had also been seriously damaged. A third F-105 strike

Peter Giroux in the B-52 cell saw the first missile just miss the leading bomber, but "a second or two later I saw a second SAM light up the overcast almost directly below the F-105. It popped through the clouds and almost immediately struck the underside of the 'Thud'. The ejection seats went out seconds later, and I was surprised that I could see them fire at this distance". Maj Norbert Maier and Capt Kenneth Theate ejected and were recovered after a hair-raising duel between rescue forces and North Vietnamese Army (NVA) troops.

In 1966–68 the *Weasels'* primary weapon was the Shrike, and with Soviet guidance the SA-2 operators learned to defeat it. Their primary defense was simply to turn off

persuaded a tanker pilot to come north and meet up with Bodenhammer, rather than see him eject. A quick calculation convinced the *Weasel* crew that they could just get to Udorn RTAFB, and they effectively glided the F-105F for 70 miles, landing with a zero reading on the fuel gauge. For a mission that Harry Johnson described as "a full day's work", Maj Thorsness was later awarded the Medal of Honor and Capt Johnson the Air Force Cross.

Eleven days later, on the 93rd mission for Maj Thorsness and his second that day, things went very wrong for his "Carbine" flight. With communications drowned out by a malfunctioning emergency beeper in an F-105's ejection seat, his element was jumped from below by a 921st Fighter Regiment MiG-21 flight led by VPAF ace Nguyen Van Coc. Thorsness' wingman, 1Lt Robert Abbott, was shot down in F-105D 59-1726 and Thorsness' F-105F (62-4447) took an "Atoll" missile, fired by Le Trong Huyen, in its tailpipe. Badly injured in an ejection at almost 600 knots, and filled with a sense of failure, Thorsness landed hard with a damaged parachute. He and Johnson were soon captured. Thus began an agonizing, but heroic, six-year prison sentence in Hanoi.

Finally released in March 1973, Thorsness received his Medal of Honor from President Richard Nixon on October 15, 1973 – his receipt of this award was kept secret while he was a PoW as there were concerns that the North Vietnamese would use this against him. Unable to return to fighters because of the back injuries he suffered in his ejection, Thorsness retired from the USAF with the rank of colonel. He subsequently served as director of civic affairs for Litton Industries, prior to taking full retirement.

flight ("Nitro") was vectored in to provide further cover, and Majs Jack Hunt and Ted Tolman each shot down a MiG. However, "Panda 03" (Capt Howard Bodenhammer) became separated in the dogfight and had only 600lbs of fuel remaining. Despite his own fuel shortage Thorsness

the "Fan Song", denying the Shrike its target. Missile crews also realised that they could track incoming *Weasels* on radar, watching for one to pull up into a climb to "loft" a Shrike at them and then turn off the radar. They realised too that the Shrike's exhaust gases contained tiny metal fragments from its solid rocket fuel. These gave a strong enough radar trace to provide warning of an incoming missile. Combined with the "dummy load" power switch described earlier, these techniques severely reduced the Shrike's chances of a kill, particularly from long range. They also frustrated dummy attacks on sites by *Weasel* crews who were attempting to force the radar off the air through the threat of a Shrike launch.

It was also clear that multiple Shrike launches did not improve the missile's success rate either. However, as a 1973 USAF Security Report concluded, "By their very presence, these aircraft reduced SAM firing rates considerably, and sometimes by as much as 90 per cent". Col James McCarthy, leading a wave of *Linebacker II* B-52s, reported "About ten seconds prior to bombs away we observed a Shrike being fired, low and forward of our nose. Five seconds later several SAM signals dropped off the air and the EW (ECM operator) reported they were no longer a threat to our aircraft". By Night 4 of the campaign, most SA-2s were manually guided, sometimes with range information from I-band signals from "Fire Can" radars, and most missiles were fired at bombers within ten miles of the sites, at two- to three-second intervals. New consignments of ARMs were tuned to operate in I-band.

Training for the early *Wild Weasel* crews was minimal. Capt Ed Sandelius was the only TAC EWO in the pioneering 469th TFS at first:

SAC had about 85 per cent of the EWOs and electronic warfare equipment. We were all trained EWOs, so the receivers were a piece of cake. The AN/APR-25/26 provided relative bearing. With practice you could interpret relative signal amplitude and get quite good at estimating range. When you flew over a site, the signal's amplitude would get extremely long and switch from 360 to 180 degrees. At this time you would try to pick up the site visually.

Wild Weasel I pilot Capt Allen Lamb added:

There was no training to speak of for *Wild Weasel I*. We did run against the SADS-1 "Fan Song" simulator at Eglin AFB to check the accuracy of the equipment. Then we went to war to see if it would really work.

The length of the strobe indication on the RWR scope showed how close the "Fan Song" was. If it reached the first or second concentric ring there was little immediate danger, but a "three ringer", reaching the outer ring, represented a real threat.

The learning curve was still rising when Dan Barry began F-105F/G missions in 1970:

On my first tour at Takhli with the 44th TFS we had a "combat tips book" full of various combat lessons learned by "Thud" pilots ahead of us. One had to do with evading a SAM at night, and the author had written, "Imagine yourself in a huge parking lot in the dark of night and a motorcycle is coming at you at maximum speed. Because there is only a single headlight you have no gauge for distance or closure rate to know when to jump out of the way. You just have to guts it out because if you move too soon he corrects and nails you. If you jump too late he's tracked you all the way to the kill. You only have one chance and you have to do it right".

In Capt Terry Gelonick's experience, "Even though they zigzagged on their upward flight, we had been briefed that if a SAM was tracking our aircraft it would maintain its same relative position on the cockpit window".

Wild Weasel crews had to face a multitude of threats, including MiGs that were usually coordinated with AAA and SA-2s. Of the 23 F-105s shot down by VPAF pilots, with the loss of ten USAF aircrew, six were *Iron Hand* or *Weasel* two-seaters. Only one was an F-105G, lost on May 11, 1972 during an *Iron Hand* mission near Hanoi. Two SA-2 batteries were ordered to fire six missiles at the flight as it moved in on a third site. While the F-105G crew (Majs Bill Talley and Jim Padgett) were fully occupied in defeating the SAMs, they did not see a MiG-21 flight closing in behind them. Their aircraft, 62-4424 *Tyler Rose* of the 17th *Wild Weasel* Squadron (WWS), was hit by an "Atoll" missile from Ngo Duy Thu's MiG-21.

Maj Talley, on his 183rd mission and third combat tour, had made an emergency landing at Da Nang after a compressor fire ten days previously and thought that he had another failed turbine. He slowed to 350 knots and ejected with Padgett (on his 13th mission) at 1,000ft. "I landed on the side of a mountain and climbed to the top to await rescue", Talley explained. "However, the rescue attempt was not made until mid-morning of the following day. I was captured just as the rescuers flew into the area where I was hiding. They tried to rescue my back-seater but were driven away by MiGs".

OPPOSITE LEFT
Capt Merle Dethlefsen displays the 354th TFS "100 Missions" banner as armorers work on his F-105F. The name of the squadron commander, Lt Col (later Lt Gen) Philip Gast, appears at the very top of the banner. He flew with the 355th TFW for a year from July 1966, completing 101 missions over North Vietnam and scoring a MiG-17 kill. He was Takhli strike force leader on the Thai Nguyen mission for which Capt Dethlefsen was awarded the Medal of Honor, and it was he who initiated the award procedure with Maj Hal Bingaman, who observed that Dethlefsen "did not fit the stereotype of the flamboyant fighter pilot". (USAF)

OPPOSITE RIGHT
Capt Mike Gilroy arrived at Takhli on July 4, 1966, following just six weeks' *Wild Weasel* training at Nellis AFB. He flew two combat tours totaling 119 missions, richly deserving his "SAM Slayer" patch (worn beneath his name tag) and the credit for his "instant inputs" and vital teamwork that was an important part of the March 10, 1967 Medal of Honor mission with Capt Dethlefsen. Capt Gilroy was awarded the Air Force Cross for his part in the sortie. (USAF)

This F-105F's front canopy rail displays Capt Don Kilgus' unconfirmed MiG kill from his F-100 Super Sabre tour in 1965. He also completed an O-1 FAC tour before converting to the F-105. Teamed with Capt Ted Lowry and this, their assigned F-105F (63-8319, which was later named *Sinister Vampire*), Kilgus also undertook a 44th TFS *Wild Weasel* tour and became a "Son Tay Raider" with the 6010th WWS on November 20, 1970. Their *Weasel* flight supported that sadly unsuccessful PoW rescue attempt, but Kilgus and Lowry were forced to eject from F-105G 62-4436 when the aircraft's shrapnel-holed fuel tanks drained dry. The aircraft had been successfully targeted by an SA-2. (USAF)

Engine failure was another occupational hazard for Thunderchief crews as their J75s struggled with frequent over-work. Engine fires were common. Indeed, 31 aircraft – half of the wartime non-combat casualties – were lost to engine or oil system problems, including eight *Weasels*. Fortunately, all were over Thai territory, although five pilots died in these accidents. Above all, *Weasel* crews learned to cope with the unexpected.

While *Weasel* crews fought in Vietnam, the training and development programs continued at "*Wild Weasel* College" with the 66th FWS/ 57th FWW at Nellis AFB. This unit replaced the 4537th FWS in October 1969, which in turn replaced the USAF Fighter Weapons School from September 1, 1966. F-105F 62-4438 (unofficially dubbed an "EF-105F") performed both training and test and evaluation functions with all these units, remaining in USAF service until mid-1983. (USAF)

For example, after knocking out several "Fan Songs" on July 29, 1972, an *Iron Hand* flight on its way home was caught by a MiG-21. As they turned to avoid its "Atoll" missile, Majs T. J. Coady and H. F. Murphy jettisoned their centerline tank, which wrapped itself around the F-105G's wing, shorted wires in the AGM-78 pylon and fired the missile towards US Navy ships off-shore! As the vessels closed down their radars, the F-105G (62-4443) refueled in afterburner and headed for Da Nang. Sadly, the errant tank prevented the main landing gear from extending and the crew had to eject.

The complexity and physical duress of the F-105G's cockpit in the days before automation could also be daunting. Dan Barry recalled:

In the summer of 1972 I was flying a night B-52 support mission at the western end of the DMZ with my "Bear", John Forrester. Just about the B-52s' time-on-target, without any RHAW signals, three SAMs started coming off the launchers about ten miles in front of us. In the blackness I immediately picked them up visually and we simultaneously started receiving their guidance signals. John started calling, "Give me the big one!" I had a Shrike selected since I usually preferred to monitor its audio signal, so I had to start switching to the AGM-78 instead while maneuvering to get the SAMs out at "two o'clock" and pushing the nose down to get our Mach up for evasive maneuvering.

The cramped interior of a 77th Battalion "Fan Song B" van, with the range, elevation and azimuth tracking operators seated on the left with their control wheels, and the fire control officer on the right. The UV van contained the seven-man crew and their radarscopes, missile control and a target plotting board. The AV van housed the electronics components for the "Fan Song", including analogue tracking computers, radar processors and uplink transmitters. Power came from a separate RV diesel generator van. Like other Soviet radars, the "Fan Song" was simple and reliable. It used sturdy, basic components that were designed for minimum maintenance by troops with relatively low levels of technical training. (via Dr István Toperczer)

Officially recognized by the NVA as a hero following his service with the 61st Battalion, 236th Missile Regiment, Nguyen Xuan Dai operated the range tracking controls of a "Fan Song" at Hai Duong, Ha Noi and Ninh Binh.

The soldiers on his course were ready to start missile training as early as May 11, 1965, but they had to curtail their tuition on the SA-2 after only two months, rather than completing the normal nine-month course, because of increased US air attacks. The NVA crews effectively learned to operate the SAM systems in practice "on the job", studying the technical aspects of the equipment at a later date. On their first day in action – July 24, 1965 – Nguyen Xuan Dai's team shot down F-4C Phantom II 63-7599 of the 15th TFW (the first American SA-2 casualty), and later also claimed to have destroyed the 400th US aircraft credited to North Vietnam's militia.

After each SA-2 engagement, Nguyen Xuan Dai and his team would quickly take cover under nearby trees just in case their battery had been targeted by an ARM. Once the all clear had been given, they would move with the battalion to another site. The SM-63 launchers themselves would only be moved under the cover of darkness, a tractor being used to pull the 12-wheeled vehicle. Travel time depended on the distance to the next site. For example, it took soldiers two days to move the missiles from Ninh Binh to Ha Tay.

Like other types of missile, when the SA-2 was activated the first stage of the rocket propellant created a huge cloud of dust and smoke and a large explosion to thrust the missile into the sky.

Personnel manning the SA-2 sites were always prepared for action. Fortifications for the weapons were dug deep into the ground, and the transporters, computing van and other vehicles, including the radar vans, were hidden. Initially, the Soviet SAMs were supplied in an overall white finish, but during the war they were resprayed in dark green paint and camouflaged with leaves that matched the battlefield terrain. Personnel even planted trees around the more permanent fortifications to deceive the USAF.

Each launcher had five to six people on duty as loaders, while the "Fan Song" team had three troops – one operator to monitor target altitude, another tracking the position and a third monitoring range. A control officer observed when the target was first detected and then turned the "Fan Song" antenna to locate the target.

Soldiers like Nguyen Xuan Dai always felt nervous before combat, but they never thought about matters of life and death. They just tried to hit the targets, although the SA-2's most effective interception method was impeded by US jamming. American aircraft, particularly the B-52, had 15 different types of jammer they could employ, while the EW-dedicated EB-66 also restricted the capability of the SA-2. Moreover, the Americans understood how the SA-2, and its radar, worked, so many early sites were heavily damaged.

Nevertheless, the NVA was quick to find new and creative ways to attack US aircraft, using manual tracking and the three-point method. Nguyen Xuan Dai recalled that after one particular engagement his regiment hid their weapons and erected fake missiles made of bamboo framework that had been painted green to resemble a real SA-2. These attracted US aircraft and enabled the AAA units around the site to find targets easily. Five American fighters were duly shot down by AAA while attacking these fake sites.

Meanwhile, I tried to get the '78 to fire, with no luck. In the blackness I immediately picked them up visually and we simultaneously started receiving their guidance signals. John started calling, "Give me the big one!" While the first two SAMs went well below us, the third looked like it had our names on it, and for the only time in two *Weasel* tours I told John to turn on the jammers. As the missile zeroed in on us I remember gritting my teeth 'til I couldn't stand it anymore, and then pulling all the gs I had speed for and rolling into it because I knew the SAM fragmentation pattern exploded in a forward-oriented cone. I was sure it was so close it was going to detonate. When it roared past us the rocket

Pham Truong Huy recalled that in late March 1972 his 62nd Battalion moved to Quang Tri during the Spring Invasion, and it was credited with the first shoot-downs of that campaign – EB-66C 54-0466 "Bat 21" on April 2 and OV-10A 68-3820 five days later. In fact, the People's Army of Vietnam newspaper for April 5, 1972 described how an "intensely burning B-52 had fallen, broken pieces of it falling to the ground". The EB-66 pilot, Lt Col Iceal Hambleton, was recovered after one of the most extensive and costly SAR efforts of the Vietnam War, but the jet's remaining five crewmembers were killed when the EB-66 crashed near Quang Tri. Pham Truong Huy recounted with pride that he had controlled the missiles that claimed three aircraft from the same battery, which few soldiers could do well. Aside from the EB-66 and OV-10, Pham Truong Huy's battery also claimed a B-52 in the Cam Lo–Quang Tri area.

Due to the topography of the hilly areas near the demilitarized zone (DMZ), batteries could only deploy three missile launchers rather than six, and they had to be set up on land that was both partly soft and partly hard as there was insufficient time to build a firmer base. This in turn meant that when missiles were fired the launchers were unstable, leaving them damaged. With no spares available, crews had to effect running repairs on the launchers as best they could.

Although they enjoyed considerable success in 1972, missile crews also suffered painful losses when the USAF attacked their sites. One night in September 1972 Pham Truong Huy was just minutes away from intercepting a B-52 when USAF fighters located his site. Kham, one of his comrades, died in the heavy attack that followed, being struck in the head with shrapnel before he had time to

don his steel helmet. He died at his position at the "Fan Song" command computer.

A missile soldier lived and fought with his unit for a long time. Indeed, they could be separated from their families for up to seven years. They had to be very resilient and endure hardships, particularly when they moved south "into the field" in 1972. They ate on the site and often had to source water from local villages, travelling up to two kilometers just to bathe.

Ultimately, the efforts of the SA-2 batteries were duly recognized on Reunification Day (April 30, 1975), when the missile soldiers were present in force at the victory parade held in Hanoi.

SA-2 Air Defense veteran Nguyen Hong Mai (left), Professor Pham Cao Thang, USAF F-4 Phantom II ace Brig Gen Steve Ritchie and Nguyen Vinh Tuyen view *We and MiG-17*, a study of North Vietnam's air defenses by Vietnamese author Thuy Huong Duong (second from right). No photos exist of Nguyen Xuan Dai or Pham Truong Huy. (Thuy Huong Duong)

motor lit up the cockpit and the shockwave gave us such a severe jolt I thought we'd been hit. Fortunately, it had gone under us and exploded 10,000 ft above us at 20,000 ft.

As we headed back to the tanker we tried to figure out what saved us. I couldn't confirm whether I made the correct switch selections to get the AGM-78 launched, and in hindsight I should have pickled a Shrike and then changed weapon selection. We wondered if the jammer had "blossomed" the SAM radar at just the right point to confuse them, or maybe they had bad fuzing. All this happened in less than 15 seconds, and I've always felt fortunate I didn't have to rethink it in a cell in Hanoi.

COMBAT

Following deliveries of SA-2s from May 1965, the Soviet Union formed North Vietnam's first missile units. Their organization was based on existing Soviet SAM regiments, and they were located around Hanoi at short notice from June onwards after the training of local operators was abruptly curtailed in response to increased US air strikes. Sites were rapidly prepared, with 64 established by December 1965.

This tally also included a number of fake sites that had been built by the North Vietnamese so that battalions could rapidly move from location to location in a "shell

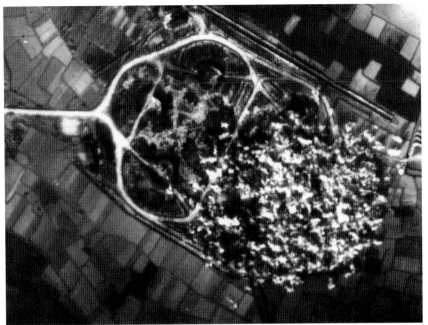

game" to escape attack. A pattern was evolved in which, as Capt Ashmore of the USAF described it, "Immediate steps were taken to establish a minimum of three alternative sites – each defended by three AAA batteries – for each firing battalion, and any of these sites could be abandoned should they become compromised".

Although this constant cycle of movement degraded readiness, it reduced the battalion's vulnerability – and clearing a site for an SA-2 battery only took four hours. The Johnson administration, alarmed at the rapid spread of SAM batteries around Hanoi and beyond, concluded from reconnaissance overflights that sites could be fully set up in only 48 hours. On September 9, 1965, F-105s flying just 12 miles from Laos and 62 miles from Hanoi were fired on by SAMs, thought at the time to be low-altitude SA-3 "Goas". They were of course SA-2s

Early SAM successes drastically influenced US planning. From late August 1965 strike packages were not allowed within range of sites without *Iron Hand* support, and for another month SA-2 batteries avoided detection from the air thanks to their mobility.

Nguyen Van Dinh, who was only 18 when he joined the 275th Regiment at the height of the air war in 1967, served alongside early SA-2 crews:

> I worked with missile troops who had trained in 1965–66 at the Baku Air Defense District in Georgia. Each regiment had trained there for at least six months. I helped the troops use and maintain the SA-2 systems and assist with weekly, monthly and quarterly checks. I was on sites when they shot down US aeroplanes and when they were attacked. Our soldiers recognized the dangers of the Shrike and could move the missiles to another site to avoid attack, although by the end of 1967 the Americans had indeed destroyed some of our equipment.

"FAN SONG" INTERIOR

The cramped, poorly ventilated interior of the "Fan Song" UV van contained the range tracker at the far end, with two other officers tracking elevation and azimuth. All had control wheels and display screens in front of them, and their roles were interchangeable.

A fire control officer sat on the right side of the van and the missile technical officer and plotter managed the tracking and launch of the SA-2s. The battalion commander monitored the "Spoon Rest" radar screen and relayed instructions from Air Defense Headquarters by telephone or radio. He received target details that were transferred to a plotting board while the "Fan Song" was warmed up – it was put on "standby" when the target was within range. Automatic tracking (possible only against non-jamming targets) could be engaged sparingly using the two trough-shaped antennas, followed by missile guidance mode along the antennas' narrow beams, but at the risk of attracting countermeasures activity. The SM-63 launchers were turned and angled to the right position ready for launch. "Ready" lights illuminated when the missiles were prepared, and when the target was in optimum missile range the SA-2s were fired at six-second intervals. In "three point" mode the tracking officers operated their control wheels to keep the target, or jamming strobe image from aircraft with ECM transmitters engaged, in the center of their individual vertical displays. Guidance information from the "Fan Song" computer was sent to the missile via its uplink antenna (exposed at the rear of the main missile body once the booster rocket was jettisoned) to keep the SA-2 within the "Fan Song's" narrow beam. Considerable skill was needed to keep the Mach 3 missile on target in the last stages of its flight, and greater accuracy could be gained from the "half correction" mode in which the missile was aimed with allowance for lead angle on the target, reducing the need for abrupt course corrections.

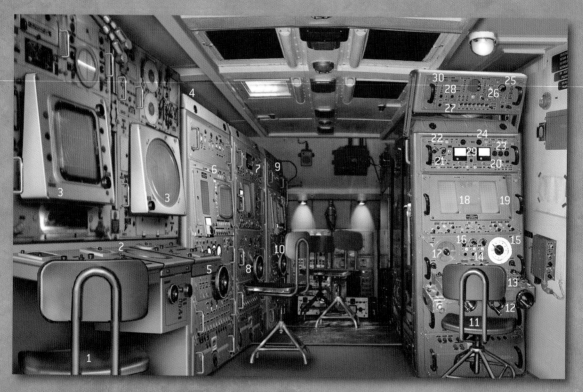

1. Battalion commander's position
2. P-12/P-18 "Spoon Rest" radar controls and goniometer
3. RH-1 scope and Plan Position Indicator (PPI) screen
4. Range tracker's console (NCO position)
5. Range tracking control wheel
6. Range tracking displays and controls
7. Elevation tracker's console (NCO position)
8. Elevation tracking control wheel
9. Azimuth tracker's console (NCO position)
10. Azimuth tracking control wheel
11. Fire control officer's position
12. Range/elevation/azimuth control wheels
13. Panel with automatic tracking and range mode switches
14. Missile firing buttons and launch lights
15. Radar azimuth dial
16. Missile guidance mode switches
17. Radar elevation dial
18. Radar tracking screen (elevation)
19. Radar tracking screen (azimuth)
20. Missile guidance radio channel switch
21. Missile fuze setting selectors
22. Missile guidance control channel selectors
23. Radar mode selectors (wide angle/pencil beam/narrow beam)
24. Live fire button
25. Missile gyro controls
26. Radar antenna deploy switch
27. Radar power button
28. Generator power button
29. Target height/distance/velocity indicators
30. Power indicator lights

As the target was approached the back-seat "Bear" monitored his ER-142 (AN/APR-35) panoramic attack indicator's three-band displays for signal activity, using his panoramic scope and attack indicator and his AN/APR-26/-36 azimuth indicator and threat lights. His view from the cockpit was extremely limited, so the pilot's vision ahead was crucial. The Shrike's nose-mounted seeker also provided the pilot with an effective radar-receiving device. Both men would listen for the high-pitched, rattlesnake-like sound – the "song" of an active "Fan Song" – from 100 miles out. Closer in, if the red azimuth sector SAM launch light came on, the pilot immediately initiated evasive maneuvers.

AGM-78s were launched as soon as there was a valid hostile radar return in order to use the missile's maximum range, as well as to lighten the aircraft. The pilot climbed in afterburner while the missile warmed up, the round then being "lofted" from a distance of between 25 and 45 miles. A green "missile acquisition" light showed that the weapon had locked onto a radar, and it was launched using the red firing button on the control column. The AGM-78's motor was ignited via a lanyard coupling, and the missile made a 5g climb before heading for the target. The crew timed its flight against the time a "Fan Song" took to go off the air, thus suggesting a successful hit.

Eleven aircraft had fallen to SA-2s by the end of 1965. A Russian technician reported that, "The most impressive moment was when the aeroplanes were downed. All of a sudden through this dark shroud an object you couldn't even see before came down in a blaze of shattered pieces".

Normally, battery commanders adhered to the Soviet rapid three-missile salvo method that was specifically created to tackle maneuvering targets. However, most of

A typical F-105F *Wild Weasel* war-load is carried by F-105F 63-8277. Element lead F-105Fs (Nos 1 and 3 in the flight) usually carried two CBU-24 canisters on their inboard pylons to destroy radar and support vehicles, while wingmen often had 750lb GP bombs. F-105D wingmen usually had the standard centerline pylon load of six Mk 82 500lb "Lady Fingers" (extended fuze) bombs to hit guns and missile launchers. This aircraft was an SA-2 victim during the Thai Nguyen mission on April 26, 1967. Hit at 6,000ft by the third missile of a salvo, it exploded, killing Maj John Dudash and consigning EWO Capt Alton Meyer to a prison camp. (Capt Paul Chesley via James Rotramel)

the early kills were against targets flying straight and level at between 18,000ft and 35,000ft. Two of the SA-2 victims in 1965 were *Iron Hand* F-105s flying at relatively low altitudes while searching for SAM batteries. Lt Col George McCleary, CO of the 357th TFS, was killed when his jet (62-4342) was hit by a missile that unexpectedly emerged from the cloud-base near Nam Dinh on November 5. Eleven days later, Capt Donald Green's *Iron Hand* flight was on the look out for SAM sites near Haiphong when a quick thinking battery commander detonated an SA-2 close to his Thunderchief (62-4332). Green, from the 469th TFS, managed to nurse his crippled jet out to sea, but he perished when the fighter crashed before he could eject.

These losses prompted new guidance to Korat F-105 crews:

Never fly below 4,500ft AGL, except when evading SA-2s. Turn into the missile and descend. "Fan Songs" take up to 40–45 seconds to re-acquire an aircraft after the lock is broken, giving the F-105 time to escape. Never fly over an undercast (cloud-base) in a known SAM threat area.

Seeing the cloud of orange-brown smoke and dust kicked out by a SAM on launch was often a pilot's best warning, but a Mach 3 SA-2 emerging from cloud after shedding its booster had a less visible smoke trail, allowing only seconds for evasion.

The extremely hazardous anti-SAM strategy known as *Iron Hand*, which was officially initiated on August 16, 1965 with F-105s, demanded the employment of new tactics. The initial response, however, was conventional. Following the F-4C shoot-down on July 24, 1965, the US government sanctioned retaliation with the commencement of Operation *Spring High* three days later. Some 54 F-105s from the 18th, 23rd and 355th TFWs, supported by a further 58 aircraft, struck SAM Sites 6 and 7, and their barracks areas, using bombs, rockets and napalm, but with disastrous results. Capt "Chuck" Horner was flying an 18th TFW F-105D when he saw "Bob Purcell's F-105 (62-4252 *Viet Nam ANG*) rise up out of a cloud of dust with its entire underside on fire, roll over and go straight in. We were doing 650 knots, carrying cans of napalm that were limited to 375 knots! I looked out to the left and saw anti-aircraft artillery lined up in rows with their barrels depressed, fire belching forth".

Capt Purcell's was one of six F-105Ds lost on that mission. Four fell to the 120 anti-aircraft guns in the area and the remaining pair crashed after Capt William Barthelmas' damaged "Thud" (61-0177) became uncontrollable near his Thai base (Ubon) and collided with an escorting F-105D (62-4298) flown by Maj Jack Farr. Both men were killed. More bad news followed, as reconnaissance photographs showed that Site 7 – manned by the 236th Missile Regiment – had been evacuated, while the "missiles" at Site 6 were fakes. Both "batteries" had been set up as flak traps in what was to become a familiar North Vietnamese tactic.

As previously mentioned, the USAF's first official *Iron Hand* strike was flown on August 16, 1965, although Maj William Hosmer had led a dozen 12th TFS F-105s against SAM Site 8 three days previously. There were no losses on this occasion, but again the site was empty. This attack preceded a short period when *Iron Hand* F-105s were placed on ground alert to respond quickly to SA-2 threats. An attack on September 16, led by Lt Col Robinson Risner, on a site near Thanh Hoa used two *Iron Hand* flights, with the lead F-105s loaded with napalm and the wingmen carrying 750lb bombs. Risner usually dropped napalm on the "Fan Song" vans while his wingman climbed in afterburner and then dive-bombed the missile batteries. On that raid two 67th TFS F-105Ds, including Risner's 61-0217, were shot down.

Iron Hand flights were soon attached to all strike missions in high-threat areas from *Rolling Thunder* 28/29 (August 20) onwards as North Vietnam's SAM network rapidly expanded. From November 1965 F-105s made low-level approaches to SAM sites with a "pop-up" climb to 4,000ft to launch 2.75in. high-velocity aerial rockets.

The first *Wild Weasel III-1* F-105Fs arrived at Korat RTAFB in great secrecy in May 1966. As a 13th TFS flight within the 388th TFW, the *Weasels* accompanied all the wing's important strike packages in hunter-killer teams (F-105Fs paired up with F-105Ds) against SA-2 sites around petrol-oil-lubricant and transportation targets. Of the flight's 12 assigned F-105Fs, only one (63-8286) was lost when Maj Roosevelt Hestle and Capt Charles Morgan ("Pepper 01") were hit by 57mm AAA during an *Iron Hand* attack on a site near Thai Nguyen on July 6. The blazing aircraft flew into a hillside, killing both crewmen – Capt Morgan duly became the first F-105F EWO casualty of the conflict.

In January 1967, the 13th TFS flew *Iron Hand* alongside 354th TFS *Weasels* in support of Operation *Bolo* (an elaborate combat "sting" that saw F-4 fighters of the 8th TFW concealed within a radiated image that simulated bomb-laden F-105s in an effort to trick VPAF MiGs into combat) and the ongoing heavy strikes on North Vietnam's industrial facilities.

Eight months later, on August 11, 13th TFS commander Lt Col James McInerney and his EWO Capt Fred Shannon were awarded the Air Force Cross for their actions during a mission against the Paul Doumer Bridge. Braving extremely heavy AAA and

F-105G FRONT COCKPIT

three SA-2s, they successfully eliminated three SAM sites without loss. This crew pioneered the *Weasel* tactic called "trolling" in which the F-105 flight flew about ten minutes ahead of the main force to search for missile sites without interference from airborne jammers. This tactic evolved into a pattern of two elements flying "figure-of-eight" orbits near a known site, with one pair of F-105s always heading towards the missile battery to threaten it with Shrikes.

The 13th TFS was a casualty when the 388th TFW shrunk to three squadrons in October 1967 due to attrition, its assets being passed to the 44th TFS, which continued the Korat *Weasel* duty until October 10, 1969.

At Takhli RTAFB, F-105F *Weasels* had initially arrived for the 354th TFS in early July 1966. Whereas Korat aircraft were assigned only to the 13th TFS, the 355th

1. Standby compass
2. AN/APR-36 threat display unit/controls
3. Reflector gunsight
4. AN/ALR-31 threat light display
5. AN/APR-36 azimuth indicator
6. Drag chute handle
7. Remote channel indicator
8. Standby altimeter
9. Vertical airspeed mach indicator
10. Attitude direction indicator
11. Vertical attitude velocity indicator
12. Ground speed and drift indicator
13. Standby airspeed indicator
14. Standby attitude indicator
15. Horizontal situation indicator
16. Pressure ratio gauge
17. Tachometer
18. Landing gear lever
19. Weapon selection switch
20. Bomb mode selector switch
21. Instrument selector switch
22. Clock
23. Exhaust gas temperature gauge
24. Oil pressure gauge
25. Caution light panel
26. Cockpit lighting
27. Landing gear position indicator
28. Bomb NAV switch
29. Antenna tilt indicator
30. Fuel flow indicator
31. Electric power supply panel
32. Bomb arming switch
33. Clearance plane indicator
34. Radar scope
35. Fuel quantity indicator
36. Fuel quantity selector switch
37. Hydraulic pressure gauge (PRI one)
38. Hydraulic pressure gauge (PRI two)
39. Hydraulic pressure gauge (utility)
40. Flap position indicator
41. Emergency landing gear extension handle
42. Rudder pedals
43. Emergency brake handle
44. Throttle control
45. Air refuel handle
46. Auxiliary special weapon release handle
47. Control column
48. Weapons control panel
49. Oxygen regulator control panel
50. Electric power supply control panel
51. Flap lever
52. R-14 radar control panel
53. Pilot's seat
54. Control transfer system panel
55. Flight controls panel
56. Command radio and AN/ARC-70 UHF short range radio control panel
57. R-14 radar control panel
58. Canopy lock lever
59. Circuit breaker panels
60. Fuel system control panel
61. Automatic Flight Control System panel
62. AN/APN-131 Doppler navigation radar control panel
63. IFF/SIF control panel
64. Auxiliary canopy jettison handle
65. AN/ARN-61 Instrument Landing Set control panel
66. Emergency pitch and roll control panel
67. AN/ARN-62 TACAN control panel
68. Interior lights control panel
69. Exterior lights control panel
70. SST-181 X-band transponder control box

TFW planned a *Weasel* flight of up to six aircraft for each of its squadrons, beginning with the 354th TFS on July 4, 1966. The latter unit's Takhli *Weasel* cadre had lost all four of its original F-105F complement within a month of commencing operations. Two of these fell to SA 2s, Majs Gene Pemberton and Ben Newsom being the first 355th *Weasel* loss when F-105F 63-8338 was hit at high altitude on July 23.

"Lincoln" *Wild Weasel* flight maintain close formation for the benefit of the photographer during Capt Merlyn Dethlefsen's March 10, 1967 Medal of Honor mission. Capt Gilroy's name appears on the aircraft's rear canopy rail, but the pilot's "name-plate" is incorrectly spelt *CAPT M H DETHLESSEN*! (Paul Chesley/USAF)

Two were shot down on August 7, as were three F-105Ds. Capts Ed Larson and Mike Gilroy fired a Shrike from F-105F 63-8358 that probably knocked out a "Fan Song", but they were then tracked by a second site, which they also fired at. Seconds after the Shrike left their aircraft they had to evade an SA-2, but a second "Guideline" suddenly emerged from cloud in front of them and detonated. Usually, successful evasion required 6,000–8,000ft of altitude above the height at which an oncoming missile had first been sighted.

The F-105's 20mm ammunition drum exploded, filling the cockpit with smoke. Unable to see the canopy jettison handle, Capt Gilroy initiated ejection but stopped the sequence after the canopy had been jettisoned. He could then see a large hole in the wing, and also noted the absence of the top of the tail fin and the aircraft's nose, but the wounded "Thud" continued to head for the coast at 500 knots. A final flak burst severed a hydraulic line, forcing the crew to eject into the sea for recovery by an HU-16 amphibian. Minutes later a second 354th TFS *Weasel* (63-8361) was hit by 85mm AAA as it took on a SAM site near Kep airfield, forcing Capts Bob Sandvick and Thomas Pyle to eject into captivity in Hanoi. This left only one *Weasel* F-105F at Takhli until replacement aircraft arrived. The 355th TFW destroyed several SA-2 sites during the rest of the year.

On December 19, 1967 a 333rd TFS *Weasel* crew added half a MiG-17 to the two already downed by *Weasel* F-105s. Majs William Dalton and James Graham (flying F-105F 63-8329 *The Protestor's Protector*) used 20mm gunfire to finish off the VPAF fighter after an 8th TFW F-4D crew had damaged it. Dalton reported that he "observed impacts on the left wing and fuselage under the cockpit" before the MiG broke away. This Thunderchief, upgraded to F-105G configuration, was lost on January 28, 1970 during an escort for an RF-4C Phantom II photographing a SAM site. At that time, "protective reaction" missions allowed escorting fighters to retaliate to ground fire. When Capts Richard Mallon and Robert Panek dived to strafe an aggressive AAA site their F-105G was shot down, and an HH-53 helicopter that tried to rescue them was destroyed by a MiG-21. Both F-105G crewmen and six rescuers were killed, the former reportedly being executed after their capture by North Vietnamese militiamen.

The AGM-45 was vital to the F-105F's SEAD mission from the outset, although crews quickly discovered that the weapon's small warhead was effective only against the radar antennas it homed onto. Lt Col Robert Belli recalled, "When we fired at 'Fire Can' radars or a SAM site we found that within 24 hours the same site was 'up' once again in the general area. We figured all they did was change the antenna".

Iron Hand jets usually flew about seven minutes (later down to just one to two minutes) ahead of the main strike package in the hope of "bringing up" hostile radar emitters and destroying them before they could threaten the strikers. A four-aircraft flight approached the target at 6,000–9,000ft and around 500 knots, dividing into two elements nearer the target – one monitored potential threat radars while the other suppressed known threats. *Weasels* tried to be unpredictable in order to outwit the SA-2 batteries, although missile crews could adapt their rigid Soviet training to keep pace with the *Weasels'* moves. Having protected the strike, *Weasel* crews waited to cover the fighters' exit, thus living up to their "first in – last out" motto.

Among the early F-105F *Weasel* pilots was Capt Mike Gilroy, who reported that SAM sites were "extremely difficult to acquire visually and looked just like the villages or jungle close by". Those pilots with luck on their side might catch sight of a dust cloud as an SA-2 was launched, thus giving them a few precious seconds to take appropriate evasive action before attacking the site.

As the CO of the 469th TFS, Maj Bob Krone played an important role in the early operational integration of the *Weasels* within the 388th TFW:

As the *Weasel* aircraft had no range estimation capability, the searching was haphazard and could not be carefully pre-planned. The SA-2 sites were invariably in heavily defended areas protecting the "hard" targets. In many areas there was more than one site within range of the *Iron Hand* flight. This forced the *Iron Hand* crews to expose themselves to the heaviest concentration of enemy anti-aircraft fire in North Vietnam, in addition to the SAM threat. The use of free-fall bombs or unguided rockets by the strike aircraft necessitated visual acquisition of the site before destruction could be expected. The necessary maneuveres to deliver these weapons also required considerable exposure to enemy defenses.

It was the consensus of pilots of the 469th TFS that the early concept of operations should have been the protection of the strike force through detection and avoidance of SA-2 sites, rather than search and destroy. With the acquisition of the AGM-45A Shrike, there was no longer the requirement for visual acquisition of the target, and the same harassment could be effected without the high degree of risk to the attacking flight. However, the weapon's small warhead, the inability of the early Shrike to discriminate and track one radar signal and the lack of an adequate tracking flare and spotting charge were limitations to effective Shrike employment.

The last two shortcomings detailed by Maj Krone meant that pilots could not use an AGM-45A Shrike to mark a target effectively, as its flight could not be followed

OVERLEAF
On the night of November 16, 1972, F-105G 63-8359 from Det 1 of the 561st TFS was flying an *Iron Hand* SAM suppression mission near Vinh, in the southern part of North Vietnam. Flying ahead of a B-52 bomber cell, pilot Capt Ken Theate and EWO Maj Norb Maier picked up radar emissions from a number of SA-2 batteries that had been moved into the area to try and shoot down B-52s. The crew set up an AGM-78 ARM, but 18 miles from the target they were suddenly locked up by a "Fan Song" radar. Maj Maier set the AGM-78 to home onto the site and gave his pilot clearance to fire. Rather than entering its usual steep climb to gain range, the missile dived down towards a SAM site and Theate entered a hard turn to the left at 18,500ft, engaging afterburner to maintain his position close to the site. Two SAMs suddenly came up through a dense cloud base that was only 3,000ft below them. The first darted towards the leading B-52 but was deflected by the bomber's ECM systems. The second detonated just beneath the F-105G, and its crew had to bail out immediately. They hid in long grass, evading capture for two nights before being picked up near the Thanh Hoa Bridge, only 60 miles from Hanoi, after a heroic SAR effort involving 75 aircraft. 63-8359 was the last of 393 F-105s lost during the Vietnam War.

visually by either the launch jet or other aircraft in the immediate area. Both areas were eventually addressed with the AGM-45A-2, which boasted a tail-mounted flare and a white phosphorus target marker within the warhead of the weapon.

When attacking a "Fan Song", the pilot had to fly directly towards the target emitter, using azimuth and elevation indicators and visual clues to identify the radar's location. Calculating altitude, speed and estimated distance from the target, he could then work out the optimum "loft angle" for the missile by using a kneepad graph. "Lofting" the missile from a 30- to 45-degree climb significantly increased the Shrike's range and dive impact, and kept the F-105 further from the SAM site. Even so, as F-100F EWO Capt Jack Donovan observed, the Shrike's range, speed and guidance limitations compared with the SA-2 made the contest "like fighting a long sword with a pen-knife in an elephant stampede"! Donovan was also credited with originating the *Wild Weasels'* long-standing motto, "YGBSM – you gotta be shitt'n me".

The 1967 Korat Tactics Manual advised that "unless the flight leader knows exactly where the SAM/'Fire Can' is located and can plan a surprise attack, it is generally good practice to initiate an attack with a Shrike to place a tracking radar site on the defensive and buy time for the flight to penetrate the critical zone between the enemy's maximum and minimum effective range".

Weasels also flew hunter-killer missions in allocated "free-fire" zones, where they could find targets of opportunity. Some of these were performed at night, often as elements divided into single-aircraft SAM hunts.

After an uncertain start (there was an outbreak of booing from 355th TFW pilots when it was first announced that pods would replace some of their bombs), all Thunderchiefs were QRC-160-1 pod-equipped by November 1966. The disastrous

Officers and troops from an SA-2 battalion in defiant mood. The Vietnamese operators, many of them conscripted college students, usually learned fast, although they sometimes resisted Soviet advice and annoyed their advisors. US pilots studied their individual tactics and respected their skills, particularly those of the Vinh battery. Others, including the so-called "F-Troop" northeast of Hanoi were considered consistently inaccurate. Some operators perfected the technique of firing from behind a *Weasel* at low altitude, reducing the jamming effect and the chance of Shrike retaliation or evasion by the F-105. For B-52 targets, track-on-jam often worked, operators using the jamming strobes on their "Fan Song" screens to provide horizontal target location (azimuth) and to give information to the SA-2's beacon, thus avoiding telltale radar emissions.

(Author's Collection)

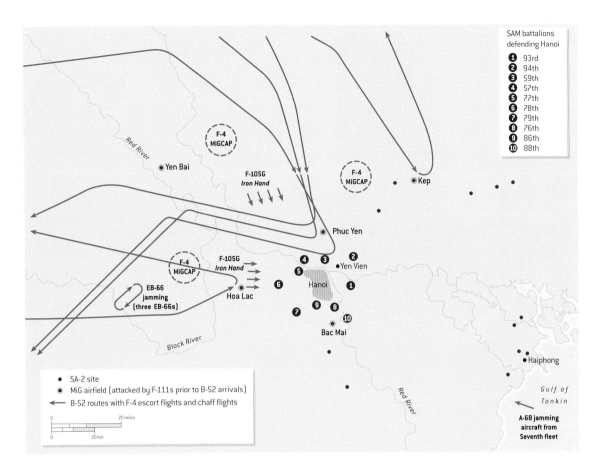

SAM battalions
defending Hanoi

1 93rd
2 94th
3 59th
4 57th
5 77th
6 78th
7 79th
8 76th
9 86th
10 88th

F-4
MiGCAP

Red River

Yen Bai

F-105G
Iron Hand

F-4
MiGCAP

Kep

Phuc Yen

F-4
MiGCAP

F-105G
Iron Hand

4 3 2
Yen Vien
5
6 Hanoi 1
EB-66
jamming
(three EB-66s)
Hoa Lac
9 8
7
10
Bac Mai

Black River

Haiphong

Red River

Gulf of
Tonkin

A-6B jamming
aircraft from
Seventh fleet

- SA-2 site
- MiG airfield (attacked by F-111s prior to B-52 arrivals)
← B-52 routes with F-4 escort flights and chaff flights

0   20 miles
0   20 km

losses (72 F-105s in the period April–September 1966 prior to adoption of the pods) over Route Pack 6 were reduced by two-thirds – North Vietnam was divided up into areas of responsibility, or "Route Packages", by the USAF and US Navy, and their strike aircraft stuck religiously to their assigned "packs". Col Bill Chairsell, commanding Korat's 388th TFW, observed, "The introduction of the QRC-160-1 (AN/ALQ-71) pod to the F-105 represents one of the most effective operational innovations I have ever encountered. Seldom has a technological advance of this nature so degraded an enemy's defensive posture".

Although most of the 72 losses were caused by AAA, the pods restricted F-105D/F SAM shootdowns to just three between October 1966 and March 1967 – 18 aircraft of other types were downed by the missiles during the same period. One of the three "Thuds" lost was *Iron Hand* F-105F 63-8262 "Magnum 03", which was trying to lure an SA-2 site into firing at it on February 18, 1967. The jet took a hit seconds after launching a Shrike from just above a 10,000ft cloud base, Capts David Duart and Jay Jensen (on their 13th mission) becoming PoWs for the next six years.

As ECM pod technology advanced, the effect on SAMs was dramatic. During August 1967 in excess of 65 per cent of the SA-2s launched lost control soon after being fired, and several crashed into Hanoi, causing substantial casualties. In mid-December 1967 the introduction of the QRC-160-8 pod, tuned to the SA-2's weak

For Operation *Linebacker II* strikes Wild *Weasel* flights were positioned to give maximum coverage to the incoming wave of B-52s and defend them from SAM sites around Hanoi. From December 16, 1972, the B-52s were concentrated in a single strike of ten waves, approaching on different routes within 15 minutes to hit up to nine targets.

The AGM-78 missile was seldom used near coastal areas of southern North Vietnam as it tended to seek out the radars of US Navy ships or American land-based radars close to the DMZ. The AGM-78C version was adapted to cope with the later I-band modifications made to hostile radars. When launched, it initially climbed to extend its range, but occasionally dived back through the *Wild Weasel* flight as it headed for its target. (USAF)

20 MHz downlink beacon signal from a small spiral antenna at the missile's rear, caused virtually all the SA-2s launched during a five-day period to lose control. And of the 247 missiles fired between December 14, 1967 and March 31, 1968, only three destroyed USAF jets. One of these was 44th TFS F-105F 63-8312 *Midnight Sun*, flown by Maj C. J. Fitton and Capt C. S. Harris, who were both killed. *Weasel* aircraft could not usually carry QRC-160 pods, as they interfered with the aircraft's other unique ECM systems. 63-8312 was hit by an SA-2 in its starboard wing, the jet disintegrating ten miles from Hanoi as its *Weasel* flight ran in towards the city.

Soviet technicians responded to the new jamming threat in two ways. Firstly, they advised the batteries to "track on jam", homing their missiles at the "cloud" of jamming surrounding the enemy formation. The second tactic was to use lesser-known frequencies available for the "Fan Song", knowing that Shrikes would thereby probably be tuned to the wrong frequency. US Navy cryptological officer Lt Cdr John Arnold, aboard the guided missile cruiser USS *Long Beach* (CGN-9) sailing in the Gulf of Tonkin, quickly "cracked" the new command codes and frequencies, however, turning the tables in the *Weasels*' favour once again.

As well as suppressing SAM sites via EW jamming, the F-105 *Weasel* flights could adopt their second, more offensive, role. As the 388th TFW Tactics Manual described it, this allowed "the *Weasel* flight to direct its entire efforts to seeking out and destroying SA-2 sites or "Firecan" AAA radars", rather than just protecting the strike force. This technique was first practiced in southern North Vietnam in 1967, but it was also used in Route Pack 6, particularly during Operation *Linebacker II*.

Takhli's first Standard ARM-capable F-105Fs went to the 357th TFS in February 1968, and the squadron made the first combat firing of an AGM-78A (Mod 0) on March 10, destroying a "Fan Song". Three of the five missiles fired on this occasion failed to guide, however. AGM-78B Mod 1 F-105Gs followed early in 1969, and they continued to support post-*Rolling Thunder* missions in Laos until the 355th TFW ceased combat operations in October 1970. The *Weasels* then moved to Korat as Det 1 of the 12th TFS, where they combined with survivors from Takhli's 44th, 333rd and 354th TFSs. Flying a mixed fleet of F- and G-models, Det 1 subsequently became the 6010th WWS, before being redesignated the 17th WWS on December 1, 1971.

The squadron participated in Operation *Kingpin* on November 20–21, 1970, when the USAF supported US Army Special Forces in an unsuccessful attempt to rescue PoWs (including 47 EWOs) from Son Tay prison. Five *Weasels* destroyed four SAM sites in the area, with a fifth one being left in a damaged state. During a later "protective reaction" strike, F-105Gs used AGM-78s to destroy the Moc Chau radar station that was directing MiG activity over Laos.

When the bombing of North Vietnam re-commenced in April 1972, the 17th WWS was reinforced by Det 1 of the 561st TFS/23rd TFW, which flew in from McConnell AFB, Wichita. The North Vietnamese had massively increased their defenses since *Rolling Thunder* had ended in November 1968, with the *Weasels* now facing more than 300 SA-2 sites. An April 16 B-52 mission attracted 250 SAMs, and F-105G 63-8342 was lost as it attacked a missile supply depot. Seven F-105Gs were shot down in 1971–72, six of them by SA-2s as Operation *Linebacker* took USAF strike packages back to the Hanoi-Haiphong area. In several cases the *Weasel* crews were just about to fire at "Fan Songs" that were tracking them when SA-2s got them first, two losses arising from missiles suddenly emerging from cloud.

However, the destruction was mutual. During Operation *Proud Deep Alpha* (December 26–30, 1971) *Weasels* fired 50 Shrikes and ten AGM-78s, knocking out five "Fan Songs" and at least three early warning radar installations.

Not all ARM launches went according to plan, as Maj Murray B. Denton recalled:

Myself and my "Bear", Russ Ober, were on a night multi-drop B-52 mission. We had gone to the tanker and were orbiting Nakhon Phanom, waiting for our next time-on-target (TOT). Russ was monitoring the AGM-78. As our TOT approached, I started to accelerate to attack speed, and selected my AGM-45 to monitor it inbound to the target. However, when the Shrike was selected the AGM-78 jettisoned from its rack! We finished the mission and returned to Korat, reporting the lost missile. Base personnel at Nakhon Phanom searched their area for two days and finally found the AGM-78 about eight to ten yards from the wing commander's accommodation trailer. On inspection, a shorted

A camouflaged SA-2 trails its distinctively-shaped tail of fire at dangerously close quarters to this gun-camera "automatic photographer". During Operation *Linebacker II* six B-52s were claimed by two sites managed by the 57th and 77th Battalions. Some sites salvoed unguided missiles in the hope of achieving a hit. (USAF)

Strike packages in 1972 used chaff flights to defeat enemy radars and F-4 MiGCAP flights to beat the MiG fighter threat ahead of the main Phantom II strike force. Hunter-killer flights, each with two missile-armed F-105Gs and a pair of F-4Es with bombs and CBUs, flanked the strikers, moving out to take on any SAM sites that posed a threat.

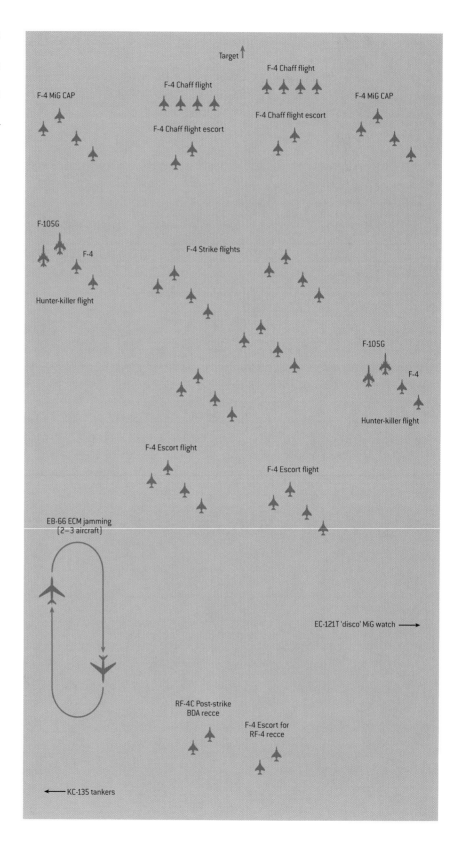

F-105G 63-8266 *White Lightning* of the 17th WWS/388th TFW is prepared for its next mission at Korat RTAFB in August 1972. This unit replaced the 6010th WWS from December 1, 1971, and continued flying combat operations until October 1974, when the survivors returned to the USA under Operation *Coronet Exxon*. 63-8266 completed another six years with the 35th TFW (visiting Germany in 1976) prior to retiring to the Mid-America Air Museum in Liberal, Kansas, in 1992. (Larsen/Remington)

and corroded connection was found on the AGM-78 pylon. Needless to say, the entire fleet was checked.

As the North Vietnamese moved south, preparing to invade South Vietnam, their SA-2 batteries followed. They shot down a 17th WWS F-105G (63-8333) from a position just north of the DMZ on February 17, 1972 and an 8th TFW AC-130A gunship from a SAM site in southern Laos on March 28. Their main objective was to bring down a B-52, and much *Weasel* time was devoted to four-hour missions protecting the bombers. "Ambush" sites were cleared in difficult terrain under Soviet direction, and batteries would fire a few SA-2s before hiding in the jungle and moving

Pre-flight preparations are underway on F-105G 62-4425, which flew the final *Linebacker II* mission on December 29, 1972, with Capts Jim Boyd and Kim Pepperell aboard. Named after Jim Boyd's wife, the aircraft's nickname became *Kloyjai* in Thai. The jet survived an extraordinary landing accident in the early 1980s when it struck the ground at a very steep angle, wrecking large areas of the rear fuselage. Fitted with a replacement rear end, it completed more than 5,000 flying hours before becoming a gate guardian outside the American Legion hall in Blissfield, Michigan, in July 1987. (USAF)

on to escape detection. After many attempts the SA-2 finally got lucky on November 22, 1972 when B-52D 55-0110 was hit near Vinh. Dan Barry was leading the *Weasel* flight of four F-105Gs that night:

> The B-52 cell was supposed to ingress from the south-southwest, and we put the 17th WWS element on the right side of its ingress track and the 651st element on the left. Since we were usually down at 15,000ft (about 20,000–25,000ft below the "BUFFs"), we never had a visual on the bombers. We operated individually in an orbit to give optimum positioning for coverage based on the B-52s' TOT. Unfortunately, they were never on our frequency, so we never received any change in TOT or ingress track, nor could they receive any advisory we'd transmit on SAM signals received.
>
> Although at least one 17th WWS crew fired a pre-emptive Shrike, I don't believe any of us received a "Fan Song" signal. I recall only one SAM being fired, and it seems to go nearly vertical before exploding at altitude. A short time later we began to hear calls on Guard frequency, with "BUFF" crews trying to make contact with one of the jets in their cell. I remember finally turning towards our egress heading and seeing an explosion at altitude and the flaming wreckage falling nearly 100 miles away.

The B-52D had managed to struggle across the border into Thailand before breaking up. All six crewmen were recovered.

As this incident graphically proved, SA-2 crews had learned how to "burn through" the B-52's considerable jamming power (particularly the less-protected B-52G) by firing in "track-on-jam" mode when the intensity of the jammers was reduced while bombers were directly above the target, or banking away just after releasing their ordnance. This technique helped them to shoot down no fewer than 16 B-52s and damage nine others during the 11-day *Linebacker II* offensive at year-end.

During this intense period of operations the *Weasels* used their missiles mainly for suppression as they orbited below the bombers. On the first night of *Linebacker II*, 47 Shrikes and 12 Standard ARMs were launched at some of the 32 operational SAM sites in the Hanoi/Haiphong area, thus keeping B-52 losses to three jets. Nevertheless, 567 SA-2s were fired during the first three nights as the B-52s flew their predictable routes across Hanoi, exposed to SAMs for a full 20 minutes. The first casualty was hit by two SA-2s fired from Nguyen Thang's 59th SAM battalion. By the fifth night missile stocks had run very low, and the 36-hour "Christmas truce" was the SA-2 assembly centers' only chance to replenish sites with more than 100 missiles.

Although only three ARMs definitely "killed" radars during the 11-day onslaught, there were 160 occasions on which radars closed down, probably due to *Weasel* suppression by F-105Gs (with F-4E Phantom II "hunter-killer" support for some missions) flying race-track patterns on either side of the bomber stream. Five sites were seriously damaged by bombs from designated B-52 or F-111A attacks, with another 15 being knocked out by F-105G/F-4E hunter-killer teams. By the last night of the campaign (December 29/30) hardly any SAM radar emissions were detected. Six more sites were hit by F-111s and two by B-52s, including SA-2 assembly facilities near Phuc Yen and Trai Cam.

STATISTICS AND ANALYSIS

Any discussion of the relative success of the SA-2 in North Vietnamese service compared with US attempts to defeat it is inevitably clouded by the "fog of war". In most cases, hits by SA-2s were observed by other crews in an American attack formation, but occasionally the speed of the interception, separation of the victim aircraft from other flight members or the wide range of other threats at the time convinced pilots that they had been hit by AAA or MiGs. "Over-claiming" was also a factor in all aspects of the air war, with several SAM sites sometimes laying claim to the same "kill", or claiming a damaged aircraft as destroyed.

However, the constant depredations of the *Wild Weasels* throughout the war steadily reduced the effectiveness of the SAMs. In 1965 SA-2s were able to destroy one aircraft for every 15 missiles launched. By the end of 1968 this ratio had dropped to one in 48 missiles fired, and the best result during Operation *Linebacker II* was one in 50, despite a huge increase in the number of SAM sites, and in the mobility of SA-2 batteries.

For the *Weasel* force the price of success was considerable. Between December 1965 and the last F-105G combat sortie in August 1973, two F-100Fs and 46 F-105F/Gs had been lost in the process of destroying or disrupting hundreds of SAM sites. Of these, seven F-105Fs and seven F-105Gs were attributed to SA-2s. In the same period the SA-2 force downed 19 F-105Ds, 15 of them in 1967 alone. Nine were destroyed in the intense attacks between October 27 and November 19, 1967 during strike or *Iron Hand* sorties at 10,000–20,000ft in daylight. Between November 17 and 19 ten of the 17 US aerial losses were caused by SA-2s. Total losses to SAMs in 1967 were 62 – by far the highest toll of the war years apart from 1972, when no fewer than 72

The Korat "Weasel" park" in January 1973, with 62-4434 (the second aircraft to be upgraded to full F-105G configuration) seen in the foreground in Det 1 561st TFS colours. "434" was also used to carry out the initial AGM-78 trials at Eglin AFB. The 561st TFS contingent was still conducting operations over Cambodia and Laos at this time, having appropriately changed the tail codes on its aircraft from "MD" to "WW" in July 1972. 62-4434 acquired the nickname *Snaggletooth* despite it lacking a sharksmouth in this view. The aircraft was scrapped in the UK in May 1996 following many years of use as a battle-damage repair trainer at RAF Lakenheath. (via Norm Taylor)

aircraft were downed in the final onslaught, including 17 B-52s. The latter was the highest loss figure to SAMs for any USAF type that year, exceeding the 14 losses of the far more numerous F-4 Phantom IIs.

Thirty-four F-105F/G aircrew members were killed in action and 22 became PoWs. The cost to SA-2 troops is unknown, but the frequent hits by cluster bombs and other ordnance must have taken many lives.

Overall, fixed-wing US losses to SAMs amounted to 205 (against North Vietnamese claims of 1,293 kills), including nine forward air control aircraft and one AC-130A to hand-held SA-7 "Grail" short-range missiles. Although this is a comparatively small proportion of the 3,322 losses (with 3,265 fatalities) to all causes, the effect of the SAM threat has to be measured in terms of its deterrence and disruption too.

The addition of SEAD flights to every strike in a high-threat area added to the cost and complexity of the missions, and diverted aircraft that could have been used to bomb primary targets. Aircraft ordnance pylons that could have carried extra bombs had to take ECM pods instead, or AIM-9 missiles to tackle MiGs. More importantly, the presence of SA-2s caused many strikes to be partially or wholly aborted as the attackers evaded interception. Indeed, many B-52 *Arc Light* missions were recalled prior to *Linebacker II*, when SA-2 sites were moved into Laos and southern North Vietnam. SAC was understandably anxious to preserve the myth of invincibility surrounding its primary nuclear bomber, and it did not want the communist world to see that its ECM protection was not completely SA-2 proof.

For the F-105 and F-4 strike packages of *Rolling Thunder*, the only defense against imminent MiG or SA-2 interception was the jettisoning of ordnance to provide the speed and maneuverability to give the pilot a chance of escape, thereby negating the purpose of the mission.

In the two peak years of activity, SA-2 sites engaged US aircraft on 1,104 occasions in 1967 and 1,135 times in 1972. However, they too paid heavily. Of the 95 batteries of SA-2s (7,658 missiles) provided by the Soviet Union, only 39 remained in January 1973, with a little over 800 missiles available – some of which were unserviceable.

For the eighth night of *Linebacker II* a concentrated wave of 120 B-52s forced SA-2 operators to use "Fan Songs" for missile guidance, exposing them to *Wild Weasel* attack. However, SAM sites were not included in the B-52 target list until the following night. This pair of SA-2s is displayed at Hanoi's Lenin Park in 1994. (Dr István Toperczer)

Two *Wild Weasel* F-105Gs were lost in September 1972, one of which was 63-8302 *THE SMITH BROTHERS COUGH DROP SPECIAL* (also named *Half a Yard/Jefferson Airplane*). It was hit by an SA-2 while flying at an altitude of 8,000ft near Phuc Yen airfield during an *Iron Hand* mission as Lt Col James O'Neil attempted to fire a Shrike at the site. He became a PoW until March 1973, but his EWO, Capt Michael Bosiljevak, apparently died in captivity. (Lt Col Jack Spillers via Norman Taylor)

Another 200 were destroyed on the ground. Although US pilots reported almost 9,000 SA-2 launches, some could have been multiple reports of the same missiles for the North Vietnamese recorded only 5,800 launches.

The growth of North Vietnam's air defense network was rapid, beginning with a few P-8 and P-10 early warning radars in 1961 and expanding to 22 sets by early 1964, with a large number of AAA guns with "Fire Can" (SON-9) and "Whiff" fire control radars to guide them. The first SA-2 site was detected by a US Navy RF-8A Crusader on April 5, 1965, and 63 others had been identified by the end of that year. This figure had risen to 150 by the end of 1966, and they were used by 30 SA-2 batteries travelling between the sites.

Despite the urgency generated by Brig Gen Kenneth Dempster's anti-SAM program in the late summer of 1965, no F-105F *Wild Weasels* were available for deployment to Thailand until May 1966. The systematic training of *Wild Weasel* tactics also began at this time too with the introduction of four-week courses at Nellis AFB's 4537th Fighter Weapons Sschool. Unlike the SA-2 crews in-theater, the early *Weasels* were using largely untested equipment and evolving tactics in situ, with a small number of aircraft and crews facing highly experienced Soviet missile operators with plentiful supplies of a battle-tested missile system.

Only 63 F-105Fs were converted to *Wild Weasel* configuration, including the two prototypes. Of these, 11 were combat losses and four were destroyed in operational accidents from a total casualty figure of 46 F-105F/Gs involved in anti-SAM activity and five during other attack sorties.

When the first F-105G shoot-down occurred on January 28, 1970, 28 F-105Fs, including two *Combat Martin* and three "Ryan's Raiders" aircraft, had already been lost, denying them to the *Wild Weasel* conversion program. In addition, around 15 jets were retained in the USA for training and test work. With a total production of 143 F-105Fs and no prospect of extra F-105G batches, the pressure on the small *Weasel* force was considerable, particularly as its intended replacement, the F-4C *Wild Weasel IV*, proved to be less capable than the F-105G.

Their sortie rates were impressive. Between March 1, 1967, and March 31, 1968 (one of the most difficult phases of Operation *Rolling Thunder*), 931 *Iron Hand* sorties were flown, 1,146 AGM-45 Shrikes were fired and 370 "Fan Songs" were claimed as destroyed or damaged. In return only two F-105Fs were lost in specific *Wild Weasel* missions at that time, but 12 other F-105Fs were destroyed in "hunter-killer" SAM attacks on 40 sites, and no fewer than 85 F-105Ds were downed, some also during *Iron Hands*. Additional to the destruction of "Fan Songs" was the even more important suppression element in the *Iron Hand/Wild Weasel* effort. USAF evaluators estimated that SA-2 launches decreased by up to 90 per cent when F-105Fs were on station.

During *Linebacker II*, in support of 741 B-52 sorties, USAF and US Navy SEAD aircraft fired no fewer than 421 Shrikes, half of them pre-emptively (to force "Fan Songs" to close down), and 49 AGM-78s against an estimated 200 SAM launchers. Only two AGM-78s and one Shrike were confirmed hits on "Fan Songs", but SAM radars were closed down on 160 occasions, reducing the destructive effect of many of the 850 SA-2s launched.

An increased use of pre-emptive launches also accounted for 320 of the 678 Shrikes fired in the period April–October 1972, when only one definite hit (and 59 "possibles") was recorded. The 230 AGM-78s fired during that period scored two definite kills and 37 possible hits, but reduced the 388th TFW's stock of the missiles to 15 by the fourth night of the campaign, increasing the need for CBU-carrying F-4Es despite heavy cloud cover on several nights. Although 380 of these launches in all were calculated as "misses", their effect in shutting down enemy radars was considered valid, reflected in the steady decline in the rate of aircraft losses to SAMs throughout the war.

The SA-2 regiments were also running very short of missiles by the fifth night of the campaign. Once sites had fired their complement, new SA-2s had to be fetched by transloader vehicles from depots that were hidden in urban areas around Hanoi and Haiphong, and there were very small stocks of ready-assembled missiles left by the end of December 1972.

While pre-emptive launching had been the basis of the US Navy's SEAD policy throughout the conflict in Vietnam, the USAF continued to rely on specialized *Wild Weasels* as a surer means of identifying, suppressing or destroying sites. In the words of the 388th TFW Tactics Manual:

> The actual destruction of SA-2 sites is normally of secondary importance in the suppression role, and would not normally be carried out unless a particular site could be destroyed without sacrificing the protective suppression the strike force requires from other threatening sites. However, for particular targets, SA-2 site destruction may be the best and most permanent form of suppression.

AFTERMATH

War-weary *Weasels* served in several post-war units, with the 128th TFS of the Georgia ANG being the last to operate the type in May 1983. They trained hard right to the end, with *Red Flag* visits and plenty of air-to-ground and missile drills that earned them two Air Force Outstanding Unit awards. Here, Mk 82 concrete rounds are loaded onto an F-105G by an MJ-1 "jammer" driver for another visit to the bombing range. (USAF)

When Congress finally withdrew funding for military activity in Southeast Asia on August 15, 1973, the 12 F-105Gs of the 561st TFS Det 1 returned to George AFB, California, under Operation *Coronet Bolo IV*, joining the 35th TFW. The aircraft remained in service with the group until 1978, when conversion to the F-105G's successor, the F-4G Phantom II began. After 17 Thunderchief years, the 561st TFS's F-105Gs were passed to the Georgia Air National Guard's 128th TFS in 1979–80. Following two years of refurbishment, the veteran aircraft flew on until May 25, 1983 when the last 128th TFS *Wild Weasel* (63-8299) was retired, thus ending 20 years of ANG F-105 service.

A second unit, the 562nd TFS, was formed at George AFB with F-105Gs of the 17th WWS upon their return from Korat RTAFB in October 1974. This squadron ended the aircraft's TAC active-duty career on July 12, 1980.

The F-105G's intended replacement, the F-4C *Wild Weasel IV*, which was scheduled to deploy to war in June 1966, was delayed two years by severe problems associated with the installation of the F-105's anti-SAM equipment within the Phantom II's denser internal structure. Despite their lack of AGM-78 Standard ARM capability, some of the 36 modified F-4Cs operated with the 67th

TFS at Kadena AB, Okinawa, from October 1969. During Operation *Linebacker II*, six jets were deployed to Korat RTAFB, claiming three SAM sites and three "probables".

Several F-4D Phantom IIs received the Bendix AN/APS-107 RHAW system and ER-142 receiver, providing crucial AGM-78 capability, but the USAF abandoned plans for 90 F-4D *Wild Weasels* in favor of the F-4E Advanced *Wild Weasel V*. With a new AN/APR-38 (later AN/APR-47) radar warning and attack system, the aircraft was able to deliver AGM-45, AGM-78, AGM-88A HARM and AGM-65 Maverick missiles. F-4Gs were among the most effective weapons during Operation *Desert Storm* in 1991, flying with the 561st TFS until 1996. The role then passed to the less capable, pod equipped F 16CJ.

The SA-2 "Guideline" continued in service after the North Vietnamese invasion of South Vietnam in 1975. Although the USSR began to replace some of its 400 S-75 batteries in the late 1970s, it continued to update the missile in many modified and refurbished variants. Whereas the F-105 was only ever used by the USAF, the SA-2 became the most extensively exported system of its kind, with more than 20,000 missiles supplied to 30 users.

The SNR-75M3 "Fan Song E" was the final production variant, accompanying the SA-2E Mod 4 missile. It added two parabolic scanners above the box-like horizontal Lewis scanner housing, providing Lobe-On-Receive-Only (LORO) capability, which greatly improved the unit's ECCM flexibility. Post-war, Vietnam continues to obtain most of its defense equipment and training from the USSR, including, in 1993, the advanced SA-10C (S300 PMU1) "Grumble" SAM.

The SA-2 was an important weapon during the Middle East wars of the 1970s and the Iran-Iraq conflict in the 1980s (when it was still in production), as well as *Desert Storm* in 1991 – SA-2 batteries were among the 600 Iraqi missile units facing Coalition strike aircraft. Finally, it played a role in the various conflicts in the Balkans through to 1999.

Egyptian forces deployed S-75M Volkhov and S-75D Desna batteries, as well as the SA-75MK Dvina, extensively during the Middle East Wars from 1967 to 1973. They were probably responsible for about eight Israeli Defense Force Air Force losses, although many more aircraft were claimed. This Dvina (SA-2) is about to be transferred to its launcher from a PR-11B transporter, pulled by a ZIL-157KV tractor unit – essentially the same combination used in North Vietnam. (US Department of Defense)

FURTHER READING

BOOKS

Anderton, David, *Republic F-105 Thunderchief* (Osprey Air Combat, 1983)

Bamford, James, *Body of Secrets – Anatomy of the Ultra-secret National Security Agency* (Doubleday, 2001)

Broughton, Col Jack, *Thud Ridge* (J. B. Lippincott Company, 1969)

Broughton, Col Jack, *Going Downtown – The War Against Hanoi and Washington* (Orion Books, 1988)

Campbell, J. and Hill, M., *Roll Call – Thud* (Schiffer, 1996)

Colvin, John, *Twice Around the World* (Leo Cooper, 1991)

Davies, Peter E., *Osprey Combat Aircraft 84 – F-105 Thunderchief Units of the Vietnam War* (Osprey, 2010)

Davis, Larry and Menard, David, *Republic F-105 Thunderchief* (Specialty Press, 1998)

Davis, Larry, *Wild Weasel – The Sam Suppression Story* (Squadron/Signal Publications, 1986)

Eschmann, Karl J., *Linebacker – The Untold Story of the Air Raids over North Vietnam* (Ivy Books, 1989)

Fitzgerald, Frances, *Fire in the Lake – The Vietnamese and the Americans in Vietnam* (Little, Brown and Company, 1972)

Geer, James, *The Republic F-105 Thunderchief, Wing and Squadron Histories* (Schiffer, 2002)

Hewitt, Maj William A., *Planting the Seeds of SEAD* (Air University, USAF, 2002)

Hobson, Chris, *Vietnam Air Losses* (Midland Publishing, 2001)

Jenkins, Dennis R., *F-105 Thunderchief, Workhorse of the Vietnam War* (McGraw-Hill, 2000)

Lashmar, Paul, *Spy Flights of the Cold War* (Sutton, 1996)

McCarthy, Brig-Gen James R., *Linebacker II – A View from the Rock* (Air War College, 1979)

McNamara, Robert S., *In Retrospect – The Tragedy and Lessons of Vietnam* (Times Books, 1995)

Michel, Marshall L., *The 11 Days of Christmas* (Encounter Books, 2002)

Momyer, Gen William W., *Airpower in Three Wars* (University Press of the Pacific, 1982)

Plunkett, W. Howard, *F-105 Thunderchiefs – A 29-Year Operational History* (McFarland and Co., 2001)

Pocock, Chris, *50 Years of the U-2* (Schiffer, 2005)

Price, Dr. Alfred, *War in the Fourth Dimension* (Greenhill Books, 2001)

Rasimus, Edward J., *When Thunder Rolled – An F-105 Pilot Over North Vietnam* (Smithsonian Books, 2003)

Rock, Col Edward T. (Ed.), *First In, Last Out* (The Society of *Wild Weasels*/Authorhouse, 2005)

Rottman, Gordon L., *Osprey Warrior 135 – North Vietnamese Army Soldier 1958–75* (Osprey Warrior, 2009)

Thompson, Wayne, *To Hanoi and Back – The USAF and North Vietnam 1966–73* (University Press of the Pacific, 2000)

Thorsness, Leo, *Surviving Hell – A PoW's Journey* (Encounter Books, 2008)

Tilford, Earl H., Jr., *Setup – What the Air Force Did in Vietnam and Why* (University Press of the Pacific, 1991)

Truong Nhu Tang, *A Viet Cong Memoir* (Vintage, 1986)

Van Staaveren, Jacob, *Gradual Failure – the Air War over North Vietnam 1965–66* (Air Force History and Museums Program, 2002)

Wilson, Tom, *Lucky's Bridge* (a novel based on the 355th TFW) (Bantam 1993)

Zaloga, Steven J., *Osprey New Vanguard 134 – Red SAM: The SA-2 "Guideline" Anti-Aircraft Missile* (Osprey New Vanguard, 2007)

DOCUMENTARY SOURCES AND PERIODICALS

388th TFW, F-105 Combat Tactics, (USAF Historical Research Agency, Maxwell AFB, 1967)

Declassified CIA Documents on the Vietnam War (University of Saskatchewan Library)

Drenkowski, Dana and Grau, Lester W., *Patterns and Predictability – The Soviet Evaluation of Operation Linebacker II* (US Army Foreign Military Studies Office, 2007)

Kopp, Dr. Carlo, *Almaz S-75 Air Defence System* (Air Power Australia, 2009)

Project CHECO Reports, including "*Linebacker – Overview of the First 120 Days*" and "*Linebacker Operations, September–December 1972*" (Directorate of Operations Analysis, CHECO/*Corona Harvest* Division, 1973 and 1978)

INDEX

References to illustrations are shown in **bold**.